HONEST
EATING

HONEST EATING

*How to Love Food,
Love Yourself &
Love Life*

Jane McClaren

CHAPEL HILL
PRESS, INC.

Illustrations by Jane McClaren

Back cover photo by Dave Dillard

PERMISSIONS

From *I Can Make You Thin* by Paul McKenna, courtesy of Sterling Publishing Co., Inc.

From *Sugar Blues* by William Dufty, courtesy of Grand Central Publishing

From *The Power Of Now* by Eckhart Tolle, courtesy of Namaste Publishing

From *The End Of Overeating* by David Kessler, courtesy of Rodale Publishing

From *Diet For A Small Planet* by Frances Moore Lappe, courtesy of Frances Moore Lappe

"Introduction," from *The Artist's Way* by Julia Cameron, copyright © 1992, 2002 by Julia Cameron. Used by permission of Jeremy P. Tarcher, an imprint of Penguin Group (USA) Inc.

From *The Omnivore's Dilemma* by Michael Pollan, copyright © 2006 by Michael Pollan. Used by permission of The Penguin Press, a division of Penguin Group (USA) Inc.

Publisher's Cataloging-In-Publication Data
(Prepared by The Donohue Group, Inc.)

McClaren, Jane.
    Honest eating : how to love food, love yourself & love life / Jane McClaren.
    p. : ill. ; cm.
    Includes bibliographical references and index.
    ISBN: 978-1-59715-069-9
1. Eating disorders. 2. Mood (Psychology)—Nutritional aspects. 3. Nutrition. 4. Food—Caloric content. 5. McClaren, Jane. I. Title.
RC552.E18 M33 2010
616.85/26   2010926500

You'd be surprised at what you can do.

ENGLISH PROFESSOR
MINNEAPOLIS, 1986

CONTENTS

In adolescence I began developing eating problems. After school during our walks home from Nipher Junior High, my friends and I would stop for a burger at Spencer's Grill, or we'd get a bag of chocolate-chip cookies from the Kirkwood Bakery. My favorite after-school snack was the chocolate-chip mint ice cream at Velvet Freeze. I found that food soothed my feelings of alienation and neglect. Pretty normal feelings for a teenager, I suppose. Food made me feel warm and cozy, that attended-to feeling of being satisfied and loved.

Coincidentally, because food served as the method my mother used to show her love, I began to develop a relationship with food, not with my mother. Food was the conduit or the means by which my mother gave love to me. It was food that I got to know, it was food that I came to love, and it was food I sought for comfort. My mother's beautifully prepared meals—the fried chicken and spoon bread, the grilled steak served with corn on the cob, and the sliced homegrown tomatoes so lovingly placed on the table—substituted for her lack of intimacy.

After every meal my father would say, "Frances, that was delicious!" We both appreciated those wonderful meals. But the food my mother put before us was carefully laid *between* our feelings, truth, and relationships. I still love food today, but now I know that a hamburger and fries don't fill a lonely gap, chocolate-chip cookies are no substitute for friends, and ice cream does not remove emotional pain.

In fact, I know—I think most of us know—that food can actually exacerbate loneliness. Overeating can isolate us, it can increase the lack of love we feel by making us feel unlovable, and it can ruin our self-esteem by emphasizing our weaknesses, bad food that is. Food has been pivotal in my life, turning from enjoying the fresh, good foods my mother prepared to abusing food by seeking any substance just to fill something missing in me. Now I am immensely thankful I have returned to knowing food as a great pleasure.

The tastes, the textures, the creativity of cooking, the varieties of ethnic cuisines, the combinations you can weave into savory meals all lead to satisfying sensory pleasures and lots of fun. In fact, nothing is more fun than good food, a good bottle of wine, and stimulating conversation around a convivial dinner table. Food brings people together, warming the soul while nourishing the body. Good food, that is.

I've always loved food, but I enjoy it more now than I ever have in my life. Ironically, while that evolution has come about, I am no longer fighting my thirty-year battle of on-and-off weight gain and emotional ill health. My relationship with food has healthy boundaries and rules, a structure I developed on my own. This structure includes guidelines such as recognizing what foods make me feel good and what foods exacerbate depression or guilt. It includes disciplines such as when to eat and when to stop eating, and where to eat and where not to eat, like in bed or in the car. It includes most of all the understanding that food is not a substitute for acknowledgment, friendship, love, or relationship.

I know my foods, I love myself, and I know my body. Most important, I've made these changes by educating myself about foods and how we digest them, by learning tools to understand and embrace just who I am, and by developing gratitude for my body and my life. I now have a healthy relationship with food—one forged on satisfaction and pleasure, not on neediness and substitution. I want to share with you what I have learned and offer you some tools and tricks that have helped me along the way.

Read *Honest Eating* in the knowledge that I love you and relate to your dilemma, your Achilles heel, a vulnerable spot we all have that leads some of us to abuse food. I hope that the information presented around my story will inspire and guide you toward personal illumination, happy health, and the knowledge that it is so much easier to have a functional life, leading to productivity and fruition, if you have a functional body.

Good luck, and remember that the journey itself delivers as much excitement and joy as does reaching our goals. Your journey begins now with every step taken, every true stone laid, and every brushstroke applied each in its own moment and each with its own sense of joy and accomplishment.

ACKNOWLEDGMENTS

I am grateful for the team that came to me through Chapel Hill Press. I am grateful for my valuable friendships, without which I simply would be less than I am today. I am also grateful for the loyal companions and sports partners throughout my life: my dogs and my horses. What is life without this sharing? And what would life be without my parents? They loved me after all.

To Linda Hobson, my editor, whose encouragement and belief in this project energized me every day: for her dedication to her profession and the tidy results that followed, I am very grateful. Edwina Woodbury at Chapel Hill Press is a genius, and I feel lucky to have connected with her. Katie Severa could not have improved upon her elegant and inviting book cover, and Bob Land so painstakingly put the final touches on my manuscript. How did I ever meet this team on this first endeavor? Through my friends Kea, Sarah, and Karen, all of whom suggested I look to Chapel Hill for a publisher. They guided me. I was very lucky.

And then my guinea-pig readers: Laura, Marc, Karen, Sarah, and Paul—all with busy professional lives—took the time to read, comment, and add value to my project. Their enthusiasm encouraged me, like a rider communicates to a horse, "You can do this. You are ready. " Thank you so much.

In my past, two friends in particular put me on a good path: Kathy, God rest her soul, saw love in me, and Janet saw intelligence and possibility. I am grateful to them every day of my life. Christine, a good friend and fellow reader, always said, "Jane, you should write." Thank you. And to my dear friend Polly, who one day when I told her that my editor said a book should entertain, educate, and inspire, replied, "If anybody can do that, you can." She knocked my socks off. Thank you.

I want to thank all my friends, who I believe love me as I love them. Thank you to: Victoria, I love your passion; Franci, whose unflappable attitude always inspires me; Jim, my true love; Pam and Fritz, we laugh; Judy and Gene, we ride; Rollin and Mariette, always wise counsel with humor; and again Sarah—who, every day, listens.

CHAPTER ONE

Calories Are Dollars in Your Pocket

L et's begin with calories: the dollars in your pocket and the fuel in your tank. If you don't know your tank's capacity, you'll have only a vague idea of what it costs to run your engine. I am five feet, five and three-quarters inches tall, and I eat 1800 to 2200 calories per day to maintain my weight of 125 pounds. Just as your tank has the capacity for only so much fuel, your checkbook has only so much money. So don't overspend and get an overdraft charge, and don't top off your tank or let the gasoline spill on the ground.

Waste, waste, waste.

In the same way, you simply cannot understand how to reach your ideal healthy weight if you're not wise to your body's caloric needs. If you waste your daily caloric capacity by eating valueless but calorie-packed foods like potato chips and sweets, that's gasoline spilled on the ground, though paid for; that's going into debt and getting an overdraft notice. So I want you to ask yourself, how can I eat and enjoy my foods to the fullest, eat as much as I possibly can to feel satisfied, yet build a healthy metabolism and get to and maintain a healthy body weight?

One answer is to avoid wasting your calorie-dollars—like the 2000 calorie-dollars I have to spend—on potato chips and sweets, for example. They have zero nutritional and energy value while they fill up your calorie-gas tank with nothing but fats and salts. You are wasting your calorie-dollars and going broke nutritionally.

Calories are like dollars in your pocket or your check-book. You have only so much to spend, and you want the biggest bang for your buck. In one day you have 2000 calories to spend without going into debt, meaning without gaining weight. Think carefully, do you want three good meals? Do you want to be able to snack? Or do you want to blow it all in one sitting? You are perfectly free to do so, but you have to pay the consequences.

Here are some examples of what I am talking about. Let's say that for breakfast you have a milkshake. This is my favorite breakfast for just about every morning:

MORNING MILKSHAKE

One frozen banana cut into chunks—this makes the shake thick and frothy

½ cup fresh squeezed orange juice

½ cup soymilk

½ cup fresh or frozen pineapple

½ cup fresh or frozen strawberries

It's simple, nutritious, and fast. My milkshake costs me just 300 calories and meets part of the required daily intake of fruits and vegetables. That leaves 1700 calories I have to spend for the rest of the day. That's a lot of calories!

But let's say I had a typical American breakfast of two eggs over easy, two sausage links, a six-ounce glass of orange juice, and two pieces of toast with butter and jam. That equals 1000 calories, meaning I've spent one-half of my day's calories before 8:00 a.m., and we haven't even mentioned fat grams and nutritional value. Believe me, my morning shake has much more health value than that high-calorie, fat-laden, artery-clogging breakfast of eggs and sausage.

Let's go to lunch. Usually we have to grab something, and here comes the difficulty. Nine times out of ten, what we might grab is unhealthy and a waste of our money—not only nutritionally, but also a waste of units in our calorie checkbook. A quick drive through any fast-food joint will have us spend from 1000 to 2000 calories: choose any sandwich, add French fries and a small shake, and we get nothing nutritionally but fat, salt, sugar, and a little protein.

How about doing a little planning to create your own lunch meals? Plus, it's fun!

SAMPLE LUNCH IDEAS

- Peanut butter and banana on whole-grain bread
- Avocado, a splash of olive oil, and a sprinkle of sea salt on whole-grain bread
- One ounce cheese or peanut butter with a great big apple

∞ No time? Then how about a small handful of nuts
along with vegetable juice?

Now we've spent wisely. Eating that peanut butter and
banana sandwich expends about 450 calories, the avocado and
slice of bread about 250 calories, cheese and an apple around
170 calories, and the nuts and vegetable juice contain about
350 calories—each way less than half the calories of a fast-
food grab, and they're loaded with protein, fiber, vitamins,
and minerals. A peanut butter and banana sandwich will
serve your energy needs instead of depleting them. Compare
the nutrition in one of these lunches with a fast-food lunch,
and you'll see that you've got a great bang for your buck.

Are you beginning to see why you need to know your calories? You want to ask yourself this: how can I eat and enjoy my
food to the fullest, get great nutritional value and energy for
my spending, and still keep money in my calorie bank? When,
at the end of the day, you've left money in your calorie bank,
you're saving calories, meaning you're losing weight. When
you spend everything you have in your calorie checkbook,

you're maintaining your weight. When you've spent everything you have and you're going into debt, you're tipping the scales and gaining weight.

Do you see the point of my saving-and-spending analogy?

Here are some comparisons to help you to gauge what foods give you the greatest energy, nutrition, and flavor while maintaining a healthy body:

Celery is a low- to no-calorie choice. Whether you have one or twenty stalks, it contains about 0 to 10 calories altogether. Add salt to taste, and you've got a great snack with lots of crunch. Potato chips, on the other hand, are the biggest waste of calories with the smallest bang for your buck. One small handful packs a whopping 160 calories, and who eats a small handful? A 10-ounce bag of just about any chip has about 160 calories per 1-ounce serving; if you eat a whole bag, that's 1600 calories—almost an entire day's worth of calories gone for nothing! Even if you just eat half the bag, you're still wasting 800 calorie-dollars.

On the other hand, 800 healthy, life-enhancing calories might look like this: one pint of strawberries, two oranges, two slices of whole-grain bread with two ounces of cheese (add Dijon mustard for added zest), and a bowl of mixed greens dressed with good extra-virgin olive oil, garlic to taste, chopped onion, champagne vinegar, and ¾ cup finely grated parmesan cheese.

See how much you can enjoy for those 800 calories? See what a waste the chips are? Celery equals 0 calories; chips equal 800 calories. See how important it is to know your calories?

Let's go out to dinner! We both like to eat a lot of food, so this will be fun. But who can have fun, yet stay trim and healthy? And who will gain weight? My dinner consists of four different items I really love:

- ✎ Halibut, mahi mahi, or red snapper seared with a little butter and olive oil
- ✎ Potatoes simply boiled, then add a little butter and fresh dill
- ✎ Swiss chard sautéed in olive oil with minced shallot
- ✎ Salad of mixed greens and minced garlic dressed with extra-virgin olive oil

I like wine with my meal but no dessert. Sweet "goo" is not how I want to spend my calories. Sometimes I exchange the fish and potatoes for pasta or filet mignon—the steak with the lowest fat content and consequently the lowest number of calories. Not too bad. My dinner totals about 900 calories, yet I've enjoyed four different items plus a good wine to enhance the flavors and the dining experience

Now my friend also likes to eat but doesn't know her calories and therefore doesn't know how to keep her calories in check. She orders the following—only three food items:

Bacon cheeseburger
French fries
Chocolate cake
One beer

My undereducated dinner partner's calories total a grand 2000 calories. That's a whole day's worth of calories in just one meal with limited tastes. Which of us gets more bang for the buck?

And what about nutrition? Well, there is no comparison. My meal offers three vegetables, protein, healthy fats, and a variety of flavors, particularly if I prepare this meal myself. When you eat out, be savvy as to how they prepare their foods. My friend's meal limits the flavors to unhealthy protein and fats, salt, and sugar, and her meal offers very little nutritional value.

The French fries are deep fried, an enemy to anyone whose goal is good health. Her bacon cheeseburger, smacking in the face of good food combining, not only renders her meal void of healthy attributes, but also is difficult to digest. And the chocolate cake will turn into unused fat, thus leaving her tired and calorie broke. Finally, since she has spent her whole day's 2000 calorie-dollars on dinner alone, she will either not be able to eat earlier in the day or for the first two meals the next day. She must choose which set of meals to forego! Rigorous starvation for the ten hours from 8:00 a.m. to 6:00 p.m. is a terrible price to pay for a fat-laden, sugar-glutted dinner—with only three food items at that!

Knowing your calories enables you to win over bad eating habits and enables you to start to understand the foods you are eating and how they work in your body. Plus, it's fun to keep a daily scorecard on yourself. Just learn the basics, and you'll find your knowledge growing in time. Soon you will know and then will be more likely to care what you are eating every day. It's a good habit to get into! And one other thing, if you stick to fruits and vegetables, our healthy complex carbohydrates, you don't have to worry about calories. Eat as much as you want!

Here are some more calorie comparisons:

- ❧ Ten radishes with a dab of butter on each = 50 calories vs. 4 ounces chips and ½ cup dip = 900 calories
- ❧ Celery sticks = 0 calories vs. 6 ounces chips and salsa = 1000 calories
- ❧ Five ounces of fish sautéed in extra-virgin olive oil, and boiled potatoes with a little butter and fresh chopped dill = 600 calories vs. a Reuben and fries = 1200 calories
- ❧ One pint raspberries and two tablespoons fresh cream = 140 calories vs. 4 ounces chocolate mousse = 400 calories (and who eats four ounces of anything?)
- ❧ Two cups of pasta Italian style (meaning not laden with heavy sauce; watch Molto Mario on the Food Channel address this) and a mixed greens salad

with vinaigrette = 700 calories vs. barbecued beef
brisket on a bun, with potato salad and coleslaw =
1200 calories.

Does $700 versus $1,200 sound like a big difference to you?
You bet it does. It's the same with calories going into your body.

Be a winner! Count your calories so you know what you
are eating and the "money" you are spending at each meal.
Understanding calories and being alert to the nutritional value
of everything you savor and ingest is fun and liberating. In the
end you will know how to eat foods that satisfy you without
guilt. No guilt? That feels great!

Take control of your calorie count, and you will take control of your eating. Empower yourself with knowledge. Learn
about your caloric needs and your ideal calorie intake each
day. In turn, you will understand and appreciate more about
yourself and your body.

CHAPTER TWO

Calorie-Counting Tricks

Now you understand the connection between calories, your weight, and your health. You understand how knowing about calories helps you understand the best use of food. Most important, you understand how wasting calories, like wasting money, can leave you tired and broke.

In this chapter I want to give you some hints and some tricks to make calorie counting easy. Soon you'll be just like me. You'll have a little computer in your head always totaling up just what you've eaten and how much it costs your body in terms of health and weight.

You'll know if you have room in your budget for that quick latte or an afternoon snack. You'll be able to plan for an indulgence because you will have your calorie knowledge behind you. So have some fun with this and see just how simple and liberating calorie counting can be. Note that all the following calorie counts are approximate.

FRUIT

Ninety percent of the time you don't have to worry about the calorie count of fruits. For instance, if you have a fruit breakfast, eat as much as you want. One cup of strawberries has only 25 calories; two oranges have 100 calories, blueberries contain 90 calories per cup, and cantaloupe has only 50 calories per cup. One-half grapefruit costs only 55 calories, so eat a whole one! And the luscious pineapple has only 80 calories per cup. Eat whatever! But be aware that some fruits come with more calories. For example, an avocado contains 380 calories, so I never eat a whole one. Just half is fine and very satisfying.

Dried fruits, so concentrated in their flavor, contain more calories than their natural counterparts. For example, one cup of grapes contains about 20 calories, while a cup of raisins contains 400 calories. Wow! And one fresh fig offers one-half the calories of one dried fig (35 calories vs. 70 calories). Ten dates cost you 200 calories. One apple is only 70 calories, while one cup of dried apple slices costs you 230 calories. So watch out for dried fruit. It is costly. And don't forget, nuts and dried fruit together are not only a high-calorie snack, they are an example of bad food combining, making it difficult to digest. (Food combining is discussed in greater detail later in the book.)

At the same time, realize that fruits are a great way to satisfy your sweet tooth. I find that when I have an all-fruit breakfast or my morning milkshake, I rarely want anything sweet throughout the day. Fruits are your friends! Eat them in the morning or for a snack, and choose natural and organic fruits when you can.

VEGETABLES

Vegetables are similar to fruits in that you can eat vegetables all day and never worry about calories or your weight. By choosing from these two food groups, you can meet all your nutritional needs for multitudes of fiber, vitamins, and minerals, and even a little protein.

So here is the trick to understanding the calories in vegetables. First, we'll divide them into three categories: salad vegetables, leafy green vegetables, and starchy vegetables. The starchy ones are the ones to watch.

Salad vegetables are lettuces such as leaf, romaine, Boston, Bibb, and arugula. Radishes, celery, cucumber, tomatoes, onions, garlic, and peppers also fall into this salad category. They all are highly water-based foods and contain very few calories, Eat lots of these and never worry!

Leafy green vegetables, all packed with loads of minerals, vitamins, and antioxidants, are also low in calories. This group includes Brussels sprouts, broccoli, cabbage, spinach, Swiss chard, collard greens, and turnip greens. They all contain 20 to 50 calories per cup. Not too much to worry about in your calorie budget.

Asparagus and summer squash are water based and light in calories, too, about 20 to 30 calories a cup.

It's the starchy vegetables you have to watch. Notice how the calories increase with the density of the food. Starchy vegetables include corn, carrots, turnips, parsnips, potatoes, and winter squashes, such as acorn and butternut. Carrots and turnips are the lowest in calories, costing about 30 calories per cup cooked. Corn, parsnips, and winter squash cost about 100 to 130 calories. Big difference. And potatoes cost about 160 calories for a 3-inch by 5-inch potato. See how the calories go up with the density of the vegetable? Starchy vegetables should be eaten with salad or leafy green vegetables. One of my favorite quick meals is a baked potato and broccoli; just heap the broccoli right on top of the potato, add a little butter, sour cream, or your favorite cheese. Yum!

Note that with all vegetables you might add a fat such as butter or olive oil. However, all fats cost 100 calories per tablespoon. So if you want that baked potato with a little butter, don't forget to add 100 calories per tablespoon in your calorie counting.

All these nutritionally packed vegetables contain from 0 to about 160 calories per serving. That's a great bang for your buck!

GRAINS

Here we find complex carbohydrates, such as whole-grain bread, oatmeal, rice, quinoa, millet, barley, and pasta. The key with this category is not to double up on your grains during the day. They cost you too many calories.

One slice of whole-grain bread contains about 110 calories. Oatmeal is about the same at 130 calories per cooked cup. Rice costs about 200 calories per cooked cup. Pasta costs you 200 calories for two dry ounces. A healthy serving of pasta served as a meal would contain about four ounces or two full cooked cups. So put pasta at about 400 calories.

Do you see how calories are increasing quickly as we move away from fresh fruits and vegetables, and how the calories in grains will add up quickly if eaten throughout the day? So be vigilant here, and watch these grains carefully. One piece of toast in the morning, not two. Skip the toast if you want pasta or rice at lunch. I eat a lot of pasta. But I do not eat pasta if, for instance, I've had a sandwich or toast in the morning. Grains just add up too fast.

> Let's review how we Americans typically eat. Starch and protein, starch and protein, starch and protein. Eggs, meat, and toast for breakfast; sandwiches and hamburgers for lunch; and meat and potatoes for dinner. That typical day might add up to a whopping 3000 calories, particularly when you consider the outrageous serving sizes we've been trained to consume.

Think! Think about calories and your serving sizes.

LEGUMES

Now let's take a look at legumes, a food group we Americans do not enjoy enough. Beans are high in calcium, potassium, phosphorus, iron, fiber, and protein—a real boon to your nutrition and reasonable in the calorie equation. All beans range from about 200 to 300 calories per cooked cup. For instance, black beans are one of the highest at 330 calories per cooked cup, a cup of cooked kidney beans contains 220 calories, and black-eyed peas the lowest at 180 per cooked cup.

Isn't that easy? Know that when you consume beans they will cost you about 250 calories per cooked cup. Just a little comparison: an 8-ounce hamburger is 800 calories. The beans will make you feel satisfied while adding lots of nutrition and energy to your health. The hamburger will likely make you tired, because you've eaten it with a bun or a starch like French fries, and because it is more difficult to digest. So don't be tired and broke. Go for the beans!

NUTS AND SEEDS

These natural food sources come from the earth packed with nutrition, but unfortunately with a lot of calories. In general, nuts and seeds cost about 170 calories per ounce. The little buttery pine nut or pignolia contains 150 calories per ounce, while pecan and Brazil nuts are 190 calories per ounce. An ounce of nuts is about a small handful or about a fourth of a cup, depending on the weight of the nut. Obviously a Brazil nut is larger and weighs more than a little pine nut, so you would eat fewer of the larger nuts. An ounce of seeds is larger, so you can eat more seeds than nuts for the same calorie count. All in all, pretty small servings for a lot of calories.

If you eat nuts for a meal, know that about 3 ounces costs about 500 calories. However, you will get a big bang for your buck—lasting energy and satisfaction. Eat nuts with vegetables and grains, or alone. They are great for a fast meal or a snack. I always have nuts with me on the road, keeping me from ever stopping at a fast-food joint. You can even pick them up at the gas station!

DAIRY, FISH, POULTRY, AND MEATS

Now we come to all the animal products, where most of us get the majority of our protein—far too much protein, some studies say. The USDA recommends we consume about 38.5 grams, or 5½ ounces of protein per day. This recommended amount is less than a few years ago and a good move on our government's part. However, that animal products are a leading cause of disease and even worldwide starvation cannot be argued, so be vigilant and conscientious about eating these once-living creatures. Use meats as a flavoring for your dishes or as a side dish—not the main course. On MyPyramid.gov, the USDA suggests that we "vary our protein routine by choosing more fish, beans, peas, nuts, and seeds"—another reason to applaud our government's attention to our health.

Do I eat animal products? Yes, I do, but not voraciously, and not without thought. I will not eat abused animals, and I will not contribute to inhumanely raised products. How do I do that? I simply do not buy from places that I think might carry such products, such as our fast-food and franchise restaurants. Certainly I never buy meat products from any chain grocery store unless proven humanely raised. When you shop at Whole Foods Market, watch for their quality standards and their new ratings on animal products. With some searching, you can find humanely raised products.

Proteins vary in calories from shrimp at 25 calories per ounce to cheese and high-fat meats, such as ground chuck, at 100 calories per ounce. To simplify, fish is generally the lowest-calorie live protein. It costs 30 to 50 calories per ounce and is your best choice for health. One egg is only 80 calories, but watch how you prepare them, and if you eat two, double your intake to 160 calories.

Notice that in this category we are talking about ounces. Just how many ounces of an animal protein does the average person eat at one sitting? A 6- to 8-ounce burger = 500 to 800 calories; a 12-ounce sirloin steak = about 960 calories; a 6- to 8-ounce chicken breast without the skin = 300 to 500 calories; a 6- to 8-ounce piece of fish = 300 to 400 calories; and 3 ounces of cheese = 300 calories. After nuts, animal proteins are by far the highest-in-calorie food choices. Unlike nuts, though, animal proteins are the most damaging to your health if not eaten in moderation. When you eat animal protein, eat it in portions of 4 to 5½ ounces per day.

Do you add a tablespoon of oil, butter, or bacon grease in preparing your meal? That one tablespoon adds 100 calories. Look to the fat content you add to your proteins, and always remember just one little tablespoon of fat is 100 calories. Whether you add mayonnaise, butter, or any oil, you are adding 100 calories per tablespoon to your daily calorie count.

Calorie counting is important to understanding what you are eating and its effects on your body. But remember: Good, healthy calories equal nutrition, health, and energy. Bad, unhealthy calories, such as sugar and animal-fat-laden foods, equal disease. So choose your foods well, sticking to lots of fruits and vegetables. Why be broke and tired when you can be healthy and invigorated?

Let's take a quick look at fast-food calories from chowbaby.com:

MCDONALD'S

Quarter-pounder with cheese	540
Large fries	525
Small chocolate shake *(Does anyone get "small"?)*	360
A quick meal at McDonald's / TOTAL = 1425 calories	

WENDY'S

Chicken breast fillet sandwich	490
Small fries	310
Diet Coke *(oh, so bad for you)*	0
A quick meal at Wendy's / TOTAL = 800 calories	

DOMINO'S

12-inch pepperoni-mushroom pizza	1812
Two of eight slices	453
One half a pizza *(Who eats just two slices?)*	900

STARBUCKS

Latte grande nonfat	210
Cappuccino nonfat venti	130
Mocha no-whip soy grande	260
Vanilla crème breve no-whip venti	790
Chai no-whip frappuccino venti	480
Starbuck's blueberry scone	460
Peppermint brownie	440
Sesame bagel	320

DUNKIN' DONUTS

Sesame bagel	380
Cranberry-orange muffin	460
Apple Danish	250
Glazed cake donut	350

PANERA

Smoked ham and Swiss	650
Tuna salad on honey-wheat	720
Smoked turkey breast sandwich	590
Garden veggie on ciabatta	570

Those fast-food calories can easily sneak up on you. *Be aware and conscious and you will not fail to be healthy.*

A myth persists that eating healthy is too expensive. Yes, it can be expensive to dine at establishments that offer clean, healthy food choices. Unfortunately for our pockets, our better and more expensive restaurants serve better foods like organically and locally grown vegetables and meats. But there are exceptions—Chipotle, for example. Steve Ellis, Chipotle's chairman and CEO, works hard to make every Chipotle restaurant carry only humanely raised animal products free of antibiotics, and in doing so has created a healthy fast-food choice. How's that for progress?

Preparing healthy food choices at home is not expensive. Look at the cost of a bag of dried beans or rice. A 16-ounce package of dried beans costs about $1.29 and has twelve servings, and a 5-pound package of white rice costs $6.25 and contains fifty servings. Do the math: the beans cost just under 11 cents per serving, and the rice is only 12.5 cents per serving. Serving ten people a pot of beans costs you pennies per person.

Add a can of tomatoes, some seasonings like chili powder or curry powder, a little garlic and onion, and maybe some green pepper, carrots, apple, or raisins to your rice or bean dishes, and you have a great variety of healthy yet inexpensive meals. These dishes yield great leftovers, too.

Compare that to a McDonald's quarter-pounder at $2.99 or Wendy's chicken club sandwich at $4.79. Then add French fries at about $1.89 and your "cheap" fast meal is starting to add up. Now add your Diet Coke at about $1.80, depending on the size, and you've got an $8.48 meal. The rice and beans with a salad might cost you about $2.00. There is always a way to eat cheap and healthy.

And compare these costs to the cost of illness. Think of the billions of dollars we spend on health care and pharmaceuticals: drugs for upset stomachs due to poor digestion and bad eating habits, medication for heart disease, drugs for diabetes and cancer research and treatment. Look in your medicine cabinet, and add up what you spend on drugs from aspirin and Tums to prescription drugs. You might be surprised at what all those cheap meals are costing you.

I have none of those drugs in my medicine cabinet, only a few vitamins. I do not remember the last time I bought a prescription drug, and I stay away from visits to the doctor by eating healthy. Healthy eating will save you and your family a lot of money. If you want to save not only your calorie budget but also your monetary budget, you can. Know your calories, know what foods tell the truth and what foods lie, know your budget, and stick to it! Remember: it's better to pay the grocer than the doctor!

—◆—

CHAPTER THREE

Getting to Know Yourself

Now we come to more challenging questions, but the answers will enable you to conquer any eating disorders you might have. Chapter 3 is about getting to know yourself.

In the ninth grade, although a beautiful, intelligent, and talented young girl, I flunked Miss Bubb's French class—a failure my parents didn't notice. I later graduated with a 1.9 grade-point average, denying me access to the schools I had dreamed of attending. All these schools had thriving fine arts schools, and all were far away from home: UC–Berkeley, University of Arizona, Sophie Newcomb, and the Artist's League in New York.

I ended up at the University of Missouri, my state's public

university, in Columbia, Missouri. It had no fine arts school; its art classes were located in the School of Home Economics. Also, I was placed in classes for the less intelligent because of my low grade-point average. Again, this went unrecognized by my parents.

I was bored, my desire to study art was ignored, and I was controlled and forced into a place my father saw for me—his place, not mine. I so wanted to be seen and acknowledged that in my confusion and lack of awareness, I grew really desperate. I began to engage in outlandish behaviors, soon earning the nickname "Crazy Jane." The name stuck, and so did the image and the consequent behaviors. I lost myself—my beautiful, intelligent, and talented self.

Through persistence I earned an M.A. in English in 1993, twenty-eight years after I graduated from high school. Now I am writing this book, and my paintings are received with high regard.

Before we can begin to change our lives, to reclaim the wonderful self we lost along the way, we want to define what it takes to do this. For instance, we want to adhere to good eating and exercise habits, but what does it take to do that? Determination and a strong will. We want to choose and spend time with good friends who encourage and support our efforts, and we want to set boundaries against those who don't: the naysayers, the saboteurs, and the nonbelievers. We will need conscious awareness and clear intent. Think to yourself what you must have in your head and your heart to get healthy. Here are the qualities, the "energies," I am talking about:

Determination
Persistence
Resilience
Optimism
Will
Resolve
Love of life

Write down in your journal whatever you think it might take to keep you on the road to a healthier life. It could be your curiosity, your intelligence, your desire, your will, or your clear intention. Now that you've made a list of these powerful tools that are available to you as they are to all of us, I want you to remember when you used one or all of them.

For example, a long time ago, I was driven by an instinctual desire. I knew I needed responsibility in my life, and I needed to share the love in my heart. Well, I went out and bought the horse I had always wanted. All my life I had wanted a puppy and a horse to love. Both were denied to me. The puppy was taken away, and the horse never materialized. These animals were not my parents' interests, and they were too much trouble for them to look after.

As I've always said, "Horses saved my life." How did I sense this need? At the time, I was so lost and going nowhere. I was twenty-eight years old, divorced, and without a career. I had no life plan, I was depressed, and my painting and the artist in me had vanished as a resource for productivity and success. Family was not an option for me. Both my parents perceived family as an obligatory nuisance, not as something precious to enjoy and develop. I got that message loud and clear. Did I even realize that I could create a successful life? No.

But I had some will, some determination, some innate desire for survival—not just survival as a lump of clay, but survival as a person with an inchoate reason for being. And buying a horse was a start—a stone laid. I had a lot of work to do before I could define more clearly what that reason was. What was the picture? What did it look like?

Having a horse in my life taught me responsibility and gave me an outlet for nurturing. For the first time in my life I had a future to plan for, in that I established goals and reached them. I had a lot to learn about riding and the care of horses. I aspired to improve and eventually went to local horse shows. I found in myself determination, persistence, and the sheer joy of reaching those goals. As the years passed, my life took on more value and purpose.

Eventually I established a nonprofit foundation to build a retirement farm and a memorial museum for our sport horses. If I had known then, in 1975, when I purchased that first horse, Telstar, what I know now—that I was worthy of success and capable of producing it—I would have looked in the mirror and thanked myself. I would have patted myself on the back and said, "Good job, Jane!"

Have you ever been so determined that failure was not an option? Have you ever persisted so strongly that winning or completion was inevitable? Have you ever picked yourself up again and again, finally to triumph over what seemed at first humanly impossible? Or are you such an optimist that failure is out of the question? Bring this picture of yourself to this job at hand, and always be able to pull up in your memory your past struggles that resulted in your achievement. Even if you recall just one such successful outcome, build on it and encourage yourself by remembering that feeling of triumph and satisfaction.

Now not only picture it; create it again by making a collage. Find your old photos, awards, degrees earned, or magazine pictures that illustrate your triumph. Paste them together in your very own trophy collage. Now paste across the collage the words, the energies, written on strips of paper that led you to your goals and your triumph. Was it determination, persistence, will, curiosity, or love of life?

I have made several collages. One depicts my persistence in gaining my degrees. I put my two university degrees, some pictures of me at school, and a picture of me receiving my master's degree on a table, and across it I added the word "persistent" written on a slip of paper. Then I took a photo of my collage. On another I put photos of my horse shows, my foundation brochures, and a picture of President Obama taking office.

Across this collage I put the words "optimism" and "determination" on top, and then took my photo of the collage.

After that I wrote how I felt looking at these remembered triumphs. I took a large piece of construction paper and wrote this: "When I look at my collages I am more aware and appreciative of my ability to sustain a dream. I feel satisfaction, and I am amazed at my fortitude and my abilities. I feel happy and capable."

I photographed this piece, too. I've kept these photos on my computer, and if I feel a little daunted by pressures or frustrated by circumstances, I pull them up, look at them, and find a new charge and new energy. They work.

Relish your glory! By looking at your trophy collage, you can re-create that power and winning feeling whenever you want to.

If you cannot recall one time in your life that you have prevailed over a hardship, imagine the feeling of surmounting something almost impossible. Imagine triumph by picturing what it feels like to scale the Himalayas or the Alps to reach the summit. Or remember seeing an Olympic hero win the gold medal. Feel the joy of a favorite sports figure or team winning or accomplishing something rare, like a hole-in-one, a shutout tennis match, a home run with the bases loaded, or a blocked goal in the final seconds to save the game.

You might look to writers who inspire you to find out how they achieved their success. Stephen King's recent *On Writing* comes to mind. It's a wonderful read and illustrates King's tenacity in overcoming alcoholism. Kay Redfield Jamison's memoir, *The Unquiet Mind*, illuminates her successful life despite many challenges. Jamison is professor of psychiatry at the Johns Hopkins School of Medicine and a manic-depressive.

Experiencing through reading about other lives, minds, places, times, and crises spurs your imagination and broadens your perspective. It's an awfully grand and huge world out there, with all sorts of people going through all sorts of trials. You can read depictions of families with daunting problems and obstacles to sort through before reaching peace, comfort, and understanding. Look to books—novels, biography, and history—for your examples, your guides, and your mentors.

After you have written down what you will need to accomplish a healthier life, and you have put together your trophy collage or scrapbook, you are ready to begin to take a good look at yourself and see, not only what you are eating, but also what's eating you. There is nothing new to this approach, by the way. This is tried and true. Most overeating—eating that is consistently out of control—signals deeper pain or suffering: bad feelings that are not being addressed, from stressful daily events to larger, more catastrophic events in your past.

How about some news that is so easy it's hard to imagine? All you have to do is recognize and accept your struggle, your Achilles heel. Most of us have one, our weak spot, signifying the pain of old hurts and old wounds. Recognize it, know it, own it, and accept it. Take some time—now—to write ten sentences about your Achilles heel. What do you want from others that you are not getting? I wanted sympathy. But who would offer sympathy to a girl whose life looked so ideal, so much fun?

What would you like to give in return? I wanted to give love, but my mother was so removed and distant, how could I? Once you give thoughtful answers to these important questions, it's pretty much downhill the rest of the way. My Achilles heel centers on the wonderful people who were my parents. Everyone loved them, including me, but I had to see, to recognize, that they were lousy at understanding me, guiding me, and just plain parenting me.

My dad made life a party. He had a zest for life and lots of luck and success. He naturally couldn't imagine life any other way. But my way was different, the way of learning about and making art, and to him that was stupid and worthy of criticism.

And my mother used to say, "I like the ostrich approach. Stick my head in the sand, and maybe it will all go away." My constant constipation as a child, a fever once so high that I saw Mother's friends leaning over me as if they were looking at me through water, my lack of interest in school, my poor grades, all were supposed to just go away. Mother's bridge games with her friends were not to be disturbed by the inconveniences of raising a child.

But in their way they loved me. They believed they would do anything for me. And they did take me everywhere with them. We traveled, and sometimes my friends joined us. I remember Polly, Kathy, and me being picked up at high school in the middle of the day to go to Florida. All our friends were in class as Dad drove us away, our hair flying in the wind with the top down. Who would imagine this lucky girl needed any sympathy?

So I grew up conflicted and lacking outlets for self-expression. I began suppressing my feelings of discontent during adolescence and simply went along with the party. My life served my parents' notion of their love for me and their light and easy social way of life, the consequence being that my future and my God-given talents got lost in the whirl.

That, in simplistic terms, sums up my Achilles heel. Eckhart Tolle, author of *The Power of Now* (1997), calls that the "isness" of life—the things that just happen. Jungian psychology might describe my childhood as the result of the stork having dropped the baby on the wrong doorstep. You see, my interests, values, and dreams didn't jibe with my parents'. After years of self-blame, feelings of victimhood manifesting as depression, and overeating to compensate for my feelings of unworthiness and neglect, I've come to be very grateful for my childhood, my parents, and my journey.

I've come to be grateful for where that stork dropped me. I got my dad's zest for life and adventurous spirit. I learned from him always to tell the truth. I watched him treat his employees with respect and saw how he established himself as their equal. He took us all through Europe and the Caribbean, and to Hawaii. He and I played golf in Ireland and Scotland. It was quite a ride, and all the while I knew his love was genuine.

And my mother was a delight to everyone. My friends loved how she listened to them and always treated them with respect. She was a great friend to others. She taught me the value of friendship, and to put other people's feelings before my own. She said, "Jane, if you can count on one hand three friends, you will have a good life." She loved cooking. Entertaining came naturally to her because she loved to have people in her home. It seems I also have that knack. How could I not be grateful?

Things happen. Who can explain them? Maybe we don't need to. Tolle says the search for understanding can become a bottomless pit. Instead, make the best choice of several ways of understanding the past. The consequences of every action and word are shaped by how you look at them—perception is everything. I guess I've chosen to look at my life with relish for the good parts. I've chosen to be grateful, and that makes me happy. But I had to learn gratitude and then establish it as a consistent habit of thinking and feeling.

Here is another exercise that helped me, along with silent meditation. Every morning before rising, look around you and thank the universe. Is it fall or winter? Do you have heat? Think of all those who don't, and thank every step, every person, and every innovation that brought you that heat. Do you have a cover over you as you sleep? Thank every source for that cover. The cotton made out of a plant, how the cotton was picked and cleaned, the design, who stitched the cover, who delivered it to the store, and how you were able to purchase it and get it home. Thank all the people and circumstances for that cover. Then think of all the people who have no cover at all.

Now after you have gone over your house, your friends, your job, the building you work in, the school you go to, and the way in which you travel around during the day, consider how you are able to work on your computer—thanking all the means and provisions for electricity, electronics, and the Internet. Are you beginning to see that your thanks are endless, infinite? Are they so endless that you are beginning to laugh at the wonder of it?

The next step is to list everything, every good deed, every helping hand you lent the previous day. You will see this list is finite. The point to be driven home is that while the universe is infinitely abundant and generous, we give back very little. Recognizing this truth is humbling and empowering at the same time.

Practice this exercise daily. Given to me by Tom, my teacher of conscious living, it was formulated by a wealthy Japanese businessman. If you continue in your practice, you will build lasting gratitude in your heart, your body, and your soul.

Gratitude powers forgiveness and action, but first there must be recognition and acceptance. It hasn't been easy to see that my parents' failure to guide and encourage me played a big part in the resulting struggle I've undergone. Recognition and acceptance might be the hardest part of your journey, too. I find that gratitude comes easier. It comes through silence and the grace of God. Some of you might want to engage a therapist as I did or a clergyperson to guide and support you through this vital journey of self-discovery. Believe me, without an honest look at the causes of your life struggle, an honest awareness of what's eating you, you will never win the battle over eating out of control.

Most overeating is done to cover up our emotional pain or stress. So you must uncover the reasons for your inner pain, then work hard to accept them as your valuable biography, your noble history. I'm going to give you some tools to help you recognize and accept the reasons for your long-term emotional pain.

Please know that we all have a foggy or darker side—that sad, frustrated, angry, lonely, and conflicted side. You are not alone in this. Accept it as a natural human feeling. By doing so you will weaken your dark feelings, your fears, your Achilles heel. See the long, dark hallway with the door slightly ajar at the end? Something sinister awaits behind it. Which is worse: obsessing about the evil, or walking down that long hall, facing it, and getting over it? Let's begin to walk together down your dark hallway.

Say, "OK, this is my life. This is the way it is. Now what can I do about it?" Maybe the first thing you can do is to love yourself enough to summon up the grit to begin a new and healthy way of living. You can do this right now, today. I'll wait while you get a healthy snack and a big glass of water. Relax and take your time, use introspection honestly, step outside of the moment, and observe yourself with objective clarity. This process is called *silent witnessing*.

You'll begin to heal as you illuminate the dark hallway. If I was able to do this—if I was able to recognize and accept my Achilles heel, and define my sense of unworthiness and frustration leading to emotional overeating—I know you can, too.

A journal, a mirror, and a calorie counter are the three simple tools you need to begin your journey toward health and happiness. Also bring along an adventurous spirit and the willingness to adjust how you've been using time. On this exciting expedition, you want to manage your time and slow it down. This process is precious, life changing, and so rewarding. So take it slow, like a very good meal: chew slowly, sense slowly, self-witness, and analyze slowly. This coming time is about reflection and self-appreciation.

Keeping a journal promotes self-discovery. Here, share with your journal every thought, feeling, and action about how you got to where you are emotionally today. The mirror serves not only as a tool for seeing yourself as you are, but more importantly for expressing self-love. Finally, a good calorie counter, whether online or a pocket-sized booklet to carry with you, enables you to understand the inevitable equation between taking in calories, giving your body energy, and the digesting and expending of that energy to look and feel great. Setting healthy boundaries, acting in self-reliance, and practicing self-reverence support our goals of self-knowledge and emotional health.

Self-knowledge breeds confidence, enabling us to know what we want from life and what we want to give to life. Self-knowledge empowers us. Our overeating stems from power-lessness and victimhood; this lack of self-reliance and self-reverence causes weak or nearly nonexistent boundaries between ourselves and others. The dangerous result makes us yearn beyond bounds for the love and praise of others. That extreme yearning makes us do all kinds of excessive things, just like I did in the ten years from ages eighteen to twenty-eight.

However, just as contractors construct a building stone by stone, and artists create a painting brushstroke by brushstroke, we can build and create our power slowly, reflectively, quash-ing the dangerous sense of our victimhood. We can do this by taking one triumphant step at a time.

Overindulgence, eating beyond satisfaction, and just plain stuffing ourselves are signs of our powerlessness. Eating for health and pleasure while mastering both is empowerment. I love Mireille Guiliano's doctor's comment in her 2005 *French Women Don't Get Fat*: "Be the master of both your willpower and your pleasure." Empowerment or victimhood, health or sickness, whole life or partial life: it's your choice. I see you have chosen health because you are reading this book, and I applaud you!

So, get together your tools for self-discovery: Start using the calorie counter for every meal or snack. Look at yourself in the mirror and say, "Hello, self! I love you. That's why I am looking at you, getting to know you, and establishing a healthy pattern for life." Then begin writing in your journal about the Four Ws: what, when, where, and why you eat.

But first, why do we want to know ourselves better? When we witness our weaknesses, witness our strengths, and realize what in ourselves promotes stability, structure, success, and happiness, we can repeat those good habits and actions. And we also can dissolve the bad, becoming stronger and healthier in the process. On the other hand, when we witness in writing what intensifies our instability, like our lack of structure in poor time management or our poor progress and resulting lack of success, we learn to avoid those bad habits and actions.

Sometimes writing about our spontaneous, habitual actions is the key to the self-knowledge puzzle. For example, why do we want to sit in front of the TV, do nothing, and just eat? Why do we go home and pull the covers over our heads? Why is it we can't wait for that 6 o'clock cocktail to feel gratified? What makes us want to disengage from life's dynamic process and be alone? Life's process is walking a road of questions and answers, challenges, problems, decisions, and solutions leading toward fruition and happiness.

Here are some possible answers to the question of why we engage in harmful spontaneous actions:

- Life's process is not something we want to engage in because of past conflicts and painful memories.
- We do not believe that we are capable or worthy of traveling along as a companion with life; we feel inadequate and downright helpless.
- Maybe we haven't really accepted ourselves; maybe we inhabit our bodies only superficially and haven't learned to love our strengths and accept our weaknesses.

∞ Perhaps our environment enforces debilitating
habits—for example, surrounding ourselves with
people who abuse food, remaining attached to negli-
gent parents or spouses, or staying in a job we hate.

Sometimes our background includes a situation I call back-
firing. Our innate survival methods backfire, go awry, or have
an unexpected and unwelcome result. We stop listening because
we cannot stand the onslaught of painful words coming from
those who are supposed to guide and nurture us. We stop feeling because we cannot stand the neglect that makes us feel isolated, lonely, worthless, and helpless. We don't plan to act in
these ways; we unconsciously stop listening and stop feeling.
But there's a good reason for this behavior. We do it in order to
survive. Most of all, we do it naturally; it is our built-in emotional survival method to use when we feel threatened.

As we grow up, we come to lack the skills to fulfill our
wishes and our dreams because of this involuntary, psycholog-
ically built-in survival method. In fact, we lose our wishes and
our dreams to a foggy lack of awareness. We lose the ability to
listen and to learn. We lose the ability to feel love or to witness

and express our feelings. As a result, we lose the keys to self-knowledge. We gave them up when we stopped listening and stopped feeling. Our natural survival methods backfired.

We can relearn the life skills of listening and feeling. We can learn these through practicing self-discovery, self-acceptance, and finally self-reliance. Empowerment develops, and help-lessness and victimhood dissolve. This is why self-knowledge, self-forgiveness, and self-reverence are what we are after.

Covering up feelings by overeating is a self-defeating act of denial of these vital changes we must make in order to live fully. Denial keeps us in the dark, looking down a long dark hallway, afraid to fully open the door at the end. If we are alive and aware, however, we see that the door stands slightly ajar. We can see a vertical line of light at the edge of the door. The answers are there in the light. Getting excited about walking down the hallway and into the light? Bring on that courage, and bring on that healthy life!

CHAPTER FOUR

The Four Ws of Your Eating Habits

So get out your journal and as you record, mouthful by mouthful and meal by meal, the what, when, where, and why of your eating habits, you will soon find yourself adding discoveries and new questions about your motives. You might write about gym class: "Today I felt so isolated and hurt in gym class. The girls made fun of me, and I am always the last to be chosen to be on any team." Write why you think that is? Are you slow because you are fat? Do you have a bad attitude and don't try hard enough? Be honest. These are your pages.

Your journal might read, "I wish my mom would understand me. Why doesn't she just listen? Is it because she's so busy, or does she just not care?" Do you really think your mom doesn't care? Do you see her life as stressed and out of control? Why is it out of control? What are the effects of this chaos on you? Write down the details of what you see, not only what you feel.

Perhaps one of your journal entries says, "My boss criticized my presentation on environmental pollution, ripped it to shreds, and that really pissed me off!" Did he see it as incomplete and under-referenced? Or did he see it as a personal slam? Or is he just a selfish, commanding son of a bitch? This is your private time and space on the page. Write it!

Use plenty of details so that the feelings of that moment can come back to you and you can acknowledge just what they are. In each of these situations, you might use food to assuage the anger, the hurt, the pain, and the isolation. See where is this going? It is a learning process about yourself. The more you observe yourself through journal writing, the more you will become aware of your feelings and why you overeat. Be specific and use plenty of descriptive details. Record just how you feel toward these daily disturbances. We all have them.

Many things initiate our need to disengage and assuage our pain. It could be a self-centered coworker who, without intending to, hurts our feelings. It could be the long drive to and from work, the stress at work, and the aloneness of our day. It could be our feeling of not getting one—not one!—kind word from anyone. It could even be aggression and cruelty that we suffer at home or at work. Observe what the triggers are, and keenly re-experience and accept them by writing about them. Notice how they bring up other stuff—old pain, old wounds, old scars left from earlier conflicts and hurts. Write wherever the memories take you, without worrying about getting off the subject. Everything is related because it's all you. Accept these wounds; we all have them. If you don't believe me, just join a therapy group. You'll hear it all!

In 1987 my oldest friend got me into a weekend group therapy session. I was apprehensive, even frightened, I guess. I felt my usual defeatist, what-does-it-matter attitude, and didn't want to go, but she talked me into it. There were twenty of us in the group. Everyone had an Achilles heel, a weak spot that enervated our life force. Then in came Jamie, telling the story of the day his dad shot himself downstairs in the basement: "My mother blamed me and told me to go downstairs and clean it up." Jamie described his reaction to seeing the remains of his father while I sustained a wallop in my gut. It was a wallop of compassion and shock at the same time. He said, "I was fourteen then, and I dropped out of high school the next year. I just couldn't keep up." My own problems dissolved, and my empathy grew as Jamie's story unfolded. These experiences teach us that we are not alone in our suffering and that our suffering is not unique.

I have a friend, Mariette, with whom I love to discuss life's process. One day I said, "Life is a gift." She responded, "I always thought life was a trial." I've often thought about that simple exchange of philosophies and have come to the conclusion that we were both right. Life is suffering. Life is also beautiful, and a healthy life is even more beautiful—it provides strength in helping us stand up to the suffering.

Through attending these group therapy sessions I learned to get help for many of my questions. The biggest ones were "Why am I so lonely?" and "Why doesn't my life work?" You may want to find a teacher, a family member, a clergyperson, a nurse at school, a mentor, or a friend to approach with your own life questions.

Another way to have some of your questions answered is to create a discussion group around this book in order to seek out people who can help and perhaps even join you on the journey of self-discovery and self-acceptance. Those of you who seek help show that you have courage. In fact, this journey toward a healthier and happier life takes a lot of courage.

It also takes resolve and resilience to get over the bumps and the hazards inherent in breaking through our denial to ask our deepest, most daring questions. It takes will and determination to not falter, and if you do fall back into depression and fear of change, to resume and carry on. But carry on you will, taking another triumphant step down the exciting and sometimes convoluted road on the way to precious you and your precious life.

Do you know that comfort food can really assuage pain, for the moment, and crunchy food can stem loneliness, for the moment? What food do you want when you just want to eat and eat and eat? Write about your comfort foods. List them all. Then read what you have written and look at yourself; look at what you tend to do again and again. Describe how you use your comfort foods and when you resort to them.

I lived on ice cream for about ten years. If someone asked me for directions, I would steer them to the Baskin-Robbins, and say,

"Then turn left at the Dairy Queen and follow Adams Road until you see the Velvet Freeze. . . ." I was obsessed with ice cream.

While living in Florida I drove to different grocery stores and ice cream shops, even if they were many miles away, to avoid the shame of facing the same counter, the same checkout gals, and buying ice cream over and over again from one store. I was eating a pint a day. That's a pint of chocolate-chip ice cream—800 calories—a day! I was like an alcoholic avoiding repeated trips to the same liquor store and hiding my shame in a paper bag. This subterfuge kept me from really looking at myself. I had become very good at building a façade of denial.

Late one evening, after a bibulous dinner party, I mindlessly headed toward Howard Johnson's for one of my favorite ice creams, their chocolate-chip mint. I entered and saw the counter service on my right and the large empty restaurant on my left. Adjacent to the counter sat the cash register with the refrigerated display underneath. I remember staring into the large, empty tubs in the glass roll-top cases. There was moisture under the glass. Very little ice cream remained in those cartons, it was so late and dreary. The place felt cold and empty, like the cartons, like me.

I remember standing and staring, not really knowing why I was there. Or did I wonder somewhere deep inside of me what I was doing? Then I noticed a basket next to the cash register holding two plastic-wrapped packages of four chocolate-chip cookies each, tied with red ribbons. I bought them both along with a remaining quart of ice cream. I got home, a miracle, took off my clothes, and put on something loose and comfortable. I sank into bed in front of the TV and ate all of it.

I still remember eating mindlessly, like a robot, but also loving the sensation, the fulfillment, and the immediate gratification. And I remember my shame the next morning. I still remember feeling sort of sick, but at the same time not sure if it was physical or emotional or what. I just felt sick. Was I lonely, afraid, or lost?

Turns out I was all of the above. Lonely because of parental obliviousness to my needs and desires, and afraid because I was thirty years old, yet out in life without any tools. I didn't know how to manage life. I was lost because I didn't know where I was, and I didn't know where I was going. The only directions I had took me to Baskin-Robbins and Howard Johnson's. I had no life plan, and I didn't know how to build one.

I still feel lonely sometimes, and afraid, and even a little lost. Call it "conflicted," but much less so. So when I want to have some fun with food, to make myself feel good and to entertain myself, I either cook myself a fabulous meal, or sometimes I just sit down with two beers and a bowl of Stacy's Pita Chips. I like the crunch, and somehow it feels fun and free, helping me to abandon my loneliness and fear.

What's different about how I do that today versus thirty years ago is this: I've walked my two miles that morning like I do every morning. I've done my floor exercises as I have been doing for the past twenty years, and my indulgences happen only once every six to eight weeks. I plan for them, and I master them.

I do my fun eating and drinking with restraint, drinking only two beers or one martini or two glasses of wine with a fabulous meal. When I am good, I eat and drink a total day's calories that never exceed my caloric reality. When I indulge, I plan ahead. If I use my indulgence as a meal, I might have a chocolate espresso bar and a latte for lunch, or Stacy's chips and two beers for dinner. I never indulge on top of my daily allotted calories, so in my meal planning I shift and insert, replacing a meal with a small indulgence. If you indulge and go over your daily caloric budget, just make up for it by reducing your caloric intake the next day.

Indulgence can be healthy, though. Say you just want to eat a lot of food. How about a pint of strawberries and a couple of oranges, the kind that open like a zipper? I love those, and they are fun! Also, create a huge, yummy salad with walnuts and gorgonzola. But avoid boring blue cheese that has been in its wrapper for weeks and tastes like plastic. Get the good stuff, and enjoy it more! Add beets, and make your salad dressing fresh, right in the bowl, because it saves cleanup, it's quicker, and it's much better than bottled.

Or make pasta, as I said—one of the best foods to overeat without overtly bad repercussions. Pasta has one of the lowest glycemic levels of the starches. The combinations and flavors you can create with pasta are endless. Be an artist in the kitchen, and create fabulously large and satisfying dishes. If you want to treat yourself with food, don't give up taste, flavor, and enjoyment. Treat yourself to a lot of really good food. Just do it with planning and knowledge.

Perhaps you prefer the really bad food indulgences, like sweets. Chocolate cake will give you nothing in the energy or nutrition area. It will make you tired and hungrier after eating it, and the pleasure will soon dissipate to sorrow. However, if you still want to indulge, skip lunch and have the cake.

Plan your indulgences, think about the consequences, and if you still want that kind of fun, make the most of it by getting the best chocolate cake in town and really enjoying every bite and every morsel. In your journal, describe eating it with gusto, the smooth, silky chocolate frosting on your tongue, and the texture of cake at once creamy, rich, and fluffy. Notice and record in detail your sensation of joy and satisfaction, and notice the fun of enjoyment.

But after just a few bites of this heavenly richness, does the taste lose its intensity and do the flavors start to dissipate? You are now realizing that the first few bites are the best, and it's the same with anything. Our palates, our taste buds, become saturated, and soon we have no taste. Soon we are just mindlessly putting food into our mouths.

- Watch out for the pitfalls of bad food indulgences:
- Eating automatically, without appreciation or recognition.

∽ Relinquishing feeling good for feeling bad.

∽ Becoming addicted to bad food indulgences.

WHAT?

What foods do you want? What foods do you crave? Line them up in columns in your journal. Keep adding to the list as you think of more foods you love.

Do you like creamy, cool foods, like ice cream, milkshakes, or yogurt? If you do, your body needs calming and coolness because of anxiety, nervousness, or perhaps stress. You might also carry heat in your body and have a high metabolism, enabling you to eat vast quantities of food. Look to Ayurvedic health practices, the ancient Hindu science and health practices for body types, and the foods most beneficial to each type. It's interesting and fun. "Pitas" like me, for instance, carry heat and like cooling foods. No wonder I lived on ice cream for ten years!

The Chinese are also aware of the body's health needs and the foods that supply them. Confucius said, "I must have ginger in every meal to aid my digestion." There's much food wisdom outside of the United States—so much that we do not understand about simple, healthy eating. Look to the Asians, Middle Easterners, Indians, Greeks, French, and Italians for guidance and simplicity, for pure, logical eating.

Do you crave comfort foods like mashed potatoes, meatloaf, fried chicken and gravy, or macaroni and cheese? You might be trying to fill some cavity, something missing in your life, like love and partnership or acknowledgment and encouragement.

Do you want crunchy food? I do. I crave salty and crunchy food for fun and pleasure. I like that I can eat it with my hands, I like the crunch in my mouth, and I like salt. A friend once said to me, "All I want to do is sit in bed and eat potato chips and drink Pepsi." Why is this? The salt, fat, and sugar all have addictive qualities. The crunch and the snap of the chips might be filling our well of loneliness, our feeling of isolation and emptiness. The noise of eating chips disguises our lack of friendship. With these cravings I think we are trying to bring back some wonderful feeling we had in our very distant past—a feeling of love, belonging, and fullness in every sense of the word.

Do you crave chocolate or sweets? Chocolate raises your serotonin level and makes you feel good for a short while. Sugar, the ultimate poison, will also make you feel good, but for a very short while. Read William Dufty's *Sugar Blues* (1986), the classic resource on all the bad stuff sugar does to you. Understand, "sugar" means white and refined sugar, that which is added to most sweets, cakes, cookies, doughnuts, icings—everything decadent and oh so sweet. It will kill you. It causes poor concentration, hyperactivity, and aggression. It destroys teeth. It leads to diabetes, hypertension, depression, and mood swings. I know that if I eat a sweet one day, I will want another the next day; it is that addictive. Watch out!

Are you compelled to drive in for a quick burger and fries? Perhaps this excursion gives you a sense of power. You drive in, order, and get it on command. The food is yours in minutes, without struggle; it's so simple, it's almost magic.

Michael Pollan, in his *Omnivore's Dilemma*, writes, "[Nineteen] percent of American meals are eaten in the car." Here's what you get: Of the thirty-eight ingredients it takes to make a McNugget, thirteen are derived from corn, including the corn-fed chicken. The rest of the ingredients are chemicals: the leavening agents; the antifoaming agents, including TBHQ, an antioxidant derived from petroleum; and dimethylpolysiloxene, a suspected carcinogen. We crave this stuff?

Powerless and uninformed people lacking control, lacking the energy and will to make an effort or a plan for feeding themselves, are easily duped by marketers for the food industry. We become pawns as we slap down our five bucks at the register for a neat white paper bag of empty and dangerous calories. The fast-food industry loves us because it can thrive on us and our weaknesses. Fast food is the perfect food for the busy, the tired, the stressed, and the servants of time. David A. Kessler, M.D., author of *The End of Overeating* (2009), sets the stage for what is to come with this comment from a food industry insider: "The food industry is the manipulator of the consumer's minds and desires."

Think of managing your time better, and make an effort to feed yourself properly. Your effort will be in direct opposition to the food industry's overall purpose. Make a daily plan that includes preparing good food. We all, at times, feel the stress of banality, meaning living in predictable and commonplace ways. We have stress because of this predictability, this tedium; as a result, many of us feel like broken souls in a mass, postmodern, and capitalistic age where just a few have all the perks and money. The trillion-dollar food industry thrives on our stress by manipulating our minds through advertising what and where to eat.

How does that make you feel? It makes me angry! It also makes me want to have more control over my health and my body. It makes me want to take back control of my food decisions from marketers paid by the food industry.

Do you love the food industry, or do you love your precious, intelligent workhorse of a body? Your body is your only vehicle through life, your precious ride that allows you to engage and celebrate life. Do you want your eating, your fueling of your body, to support big business and support its abuse of your body? Or do you want to take control of your body and your health? It's up to you.

Looking at what we eat by writing about what we eat helps us to see ourselves, our tendencies, and our habits. As I said, the motivation for our overeating is housed in our emotions. Stuffing down our feelings with gross quantities of food ensures procrastination, more body fat, and low energy. Stop putting off your journey of self-discovery, self-acceptance, self-reliance, and self-reverence. Join this wonderful dance of life by writing in your journal and listing what you eat.

As we move closer to the big question—why you eat . . . all the true, honest reasons you overeat—first write about when and where you eat, using descriptive details and remembered scenes and conversations.

WHEN AND WHERE

When and where do you eat? Answering in detail is important because it will expose bad habits that you can change, right now, today. Isn't that exciting? Thirty years ago I realized that most of my eating took place after 8:00 p.m. in front of the TV. Sound familiar? Right then and there I decided to go to bed earlier, at 9:00 p.m.

A miraculous change took place. I started to lose weight, I slept better, and I had more energy. I began exchanging a bad habit for a good habit. I stopped staying up late and eating, and my biorhythms started changing. Now I go to bed early with a good book instead of being bored in front of the TV and engaging in mindless eating.

A friend of mine once described how easy it is to eat a quart of ice cream while driving in the car. "Oh," Susan said, "it's a lot easier than you'd think. Just put it on your lap and dig in!" How can you enjoy ice cream while your mind concentrates on driving, staying on the road, avoiding the other cars, and following road signs and traffic lights? The answer is, you can't!

So why ingest 2000 calories, Susan's allotment for the day, without the slightest awareness or enjoyment? This habit is hard to break, sure, but you have two ways to do it: all at once (hard) or little by little (easier). I vote for all at once, by changing your circumstances. That's what I did. Put your purse on your lap, change your route to avoid Baskin-Robbins, or join a carpool.

Here's why you can break the habit. *If you eat while doing anything else, such as driving, watching TV, reading, or talking on the phone, recognize this fact: you do not taste the food, nor will you derive any lasting satisfaction from the experience.* You are eating mindlessly and in the controlled confines of a bad habit. Do you eat standing? That's another clue to mindless eating. Control and change your habit of eating while engaged in another activity, such as eating while standing or walking around.

Stop mindless eating. Savor and recognize your meal. Honor it, eating slowly and delighting in every small bite. Only through aware eating can you feel satisfaction, and with satisfaction you will eat less. Enjoy your food. If you do not have time to enjoy your food, take a big handful of nuts, approximately three ounces. Eat them while sitting down—ingesting about 500 calories, enough for one small meal—and boom, you're finished. They're quick and good for you.

Do you like to eat out with friends? If a major part of your calorie-dollars are spent with a friend or friends, maybe you'd better look at that friendship and that environment. Is it inhibiting your success? Do you often hear things like, "Hey, let's stop for a burger." Or, "Oh, there's a Dairy Queen. Yummy, let's go!" Or even worse, "Why worry about your weight? Life is short!" Yes, short and miserable for those out of control and ignorant of what it feels like to be healthy, energetic, vibrant, and feeling good.

Look at your environment, and be aware of any debilitating circumstances and negative friends. Then either remove yourself from the environment in question, or acknowledge the pitfalls and deal with them with resolve and composure. You have made the choice to be healthy and feel good about yourself. However, this choice is not always what everyone else decides to do, and that's OK. Just don't let others' decisions bring you down, influencing you to stay trapped in bad food habits.

I had a dear friend a while back who loves to eat. While I love to eat, too, I mostly enjoy food that is good for me. My friend, however, loved everything—greasy breakfasts, chips and gooey cheesy dip, big pizzas laden with everything, and lots of beer. I found myself eating less when I was around her because to watch her stuff herself with all that bad food made me sick. It also made me sorry for her—sad because I knew she was ruining her health, and sad because this woman was so beautiful.

Yet her outside appearance showed neglect and self-irreverence, almost to the point of self-hatred. To be honest with you, I did gain a little weight when were together in school. I loved our friendship; the indulgent nature of it all was hard to resist, but in the end the friendship just wasn't healthy. One night after way too much to drink, we had an argument. I

haven't seen her since, and I miss her still. Good friends sometimes require a self-discipline that is beyond our resolve and
our will. Good friends can be lost in out-of-control indulgences. I'm so sorry.

This personal story makes me think of another story,
a story in the limelight. While writing this book, I've been
asking myself: *Why does Oprah, with all her resources, all the
love and support, and encouragement from Bob Greene, her personal fitness guru, not lose her weight? Why can't she control her
eating habits? She could be overeating on lobster, caviar, and
champagne—hardly fat-producing items! It seems she could so
easily manage her indulgences.*

Well, I have the answer. It just might be because of her dear
friendship with Gayle King, editor-at-large for *O* magazine.
What a beautiful friendship, such love and support, such joy!
And yet the bad food the two tend to eat! Did you see them
at the Dallas State Fair? That was a food indulgence! Oprah
has said, "No one likes to eat like Gayle." There you have it,
a true environmental disaster of what, when, where, and why
for anyone who wants to control overeating. They love to eat,
and I'm guessing, together. Oprah and Gayle would have to

team up to manage their overeating, the true friends that they are. I would like to see both Oprah and Gayle around for a very long time, but I'm afraid in this food-fun environment, longevity will be hard for them to reach.

Do you like eating at parties, especially the ones where you graze and don't sit down? At these sorts of parties, do you really notice and savor what you are eating? Or are you still hungry an hour or so after? If you are still hungry after a grazing-type dinner party, it is because you have not registered in your mind any satisfaction with what you have eaten. You were eating without conscious awareness.

This little insight illuminates the power of our brains. We can actually eat enough food to fill us up without even noticing. While enjoying a party there is conversation going on, new people walking through the door, and our attention is on all that swirls around us, so we don't notice what we are eating. *Without conscious and aware eating, our brains fail to compute satiation.*

So notice your habits by writing about when and where you eat every day for a month. Read over the facts of your circumstantial eating habits. Then decide how and what to change. Change the bad habits—the ones that are inhibiting your energy, your weight loss, your health, and your complete engagement with life. We only go around once in this life, so go around now with joy!

WHY

Here's the big question: Why do you eat? Because you are hungry? Because it's the right time for a meal? When is the last time you actually experienced hunger? Sometimes we feel lightheaded and weak. That's low blood sugar, though we assume it's the result of hunger. Know the difference. A cup of bouillon, a piece of fruit, or any small snack low in calories, like a tablespoon of peanut butter, can satisfy low blood sugar. Hunger is what we all should feel upon rising in the morning. I have a saying: "If I'm not hungry in the morning, I've either eaten too late or too much the night before."

So, why do you eat: To enjoy food and to satisfy your hunger? Do you eat to celebrate a good day? I do that. Do you eat to satisfy or satiate something other than hunger? I do that, too. Many of us overeaters eat because eating assuages our stress, feelings of helplessness, loneliness, and depression.

Food and the act of eating are the two most readily available and most socially acceptable things to do in order to calm or hide our feelings of discomfort. After all, when we were babies, our mother's breast was not only our source of nourishment but comfort and safety as well. We were held close to our mother's body, giving us a feeling of safety, protection, love, and comfort all while we were filling up our hunger. As adults, can we always succeed at replicating that feeling of pure joy and love close to another person? Ask yourself, "Do I feel safe and loved now?"

If your answer—your honest answer—is "No," as it is for many of us, are you trying to find love and safety, and maybe even joy, in food? David A. Kessler tells of a venture capitalist in the food industry who told him, "Starbucks has recognized and responded brilliantly to a cultural need. . . . It's about warm milk in a bottle. If I could put a nipple on it, I'd be a multimillionaire." What does that say about the food industry's canny ability to exploit our emotional needs? It says enough to convince me.

If you recognize this emptiness in yourself, recognize, too, that this emptiness is a societal condition of our age, not your individual weakness. *Once you recognize that you are trying to fill your emptiness with food, your desire to do so will weaken.* You'll eventually master this unproductive desire if you continue to use your journal, your mirror, and your calorie counter. You will master the bad habit.

Once the hidden and underlying causes of bad habits are discovered and recognized, they are weakened. Look to Eckhart Tolle's *A New Earth*, and his *The Power of Now* for more on this subject: "No truly positive action can arise out of an unsurrendered state of consciousness." Awareness, recognition, and acceptance or surrender are powerful tools toward self-discovery, empowerment, and a life lived in the light of health. See yourself first as you write in your journal. Read it back to yourself, accept yourself as you are, and surrender to your Achilles heel. Then you can take the first steps toward positive action. Surrendering does not mean giving up; it means becoming consciously aware of yourself—your strengths, weaknesses, and habits. By the way, surrendering also means having a sense of humor about yourself.

Developing consciousness is a practice, a study, and a discipline. This includes meditation, and being present or in the now. Meditation takes from ten minutes to one hour and can be practiced daily. Just sit in silence. Being present can be ongoing, too. If you study your environment by taking notice and becoming aware of actions and words presented to you, you will become more conscious. You will become more grateful for your life.

Sometimes a moment of silent witnessing takes place, such as one time when a friend was yelling at me. I remember thinking, *This is awful! I feel as though I am being flogged and burned at the stake*. I remembered losing my temper in the past, but did not do so that day. I was reminded of the suffering such action can cause. Another time I stood back and saw myself clearly as a nurturer, one who likes to make others feel good. Silent witnessing clarifies your understanding of yourself, connects you to your environment, and promotes self-knowledge and new habits.

Listening to others and paying attention to the details of their daily lives strengthen your conscious living, too. When you are conscious, people and all other energy pays attention to you. The universe will pay attention to you. You will find pathways opening and subtle means being offered to you. This is my first book, my steps taken in positive action. I know the path to getting published is arduous at best. Many first-time authors present their work to a hundred agents and publishers before getting a commitment. However, the first publisher I sent my manuscript to introduced me to my editor, and you are reaping the benefit of that timely gift. Getting to know myself, accepting my past failures, and becoming more conscious on a daily basis have all helped me to fulfill myself. And not full-fill myself on food!

So right now, write in your journal the many reasons *why* you eat. Write this with honesty, courage, and the will and curiosity to know your precious self—now, while there's good time left. I write in my journal either before I go to sleep or early in the morning. After a good night's sleep, I find my mind to be clear and open to understanding. Plato said, "The life which is unexamined is not worth living" (*Apology*). Richness of understanding comes to a life examined and contemplated.

Last night I got home tired and feeling lonely after a disappointing day. It all started out so well, but as the afternoon dragged on I felt more and more dissatisfied. The economy had tanked, the war raged on against terrorists, congresspersons were bickering, and my horse was lame. So I opened a bottle of wine and got out some cheese and crackers and started eating. I wanted to soothe myself and enjoy myself. I had thawed a small filet mignon to really enjoy along with fresh asparagus and broccoli. All my food was delicious and satisfying.

I woke up the next morning tired and sorry that I had overeaten and drunk too much wine. *Why did I do this to myself?* I wondered. *There is no love in food; food just puts off the emptiness.* A filet mignon couldn't fill my empty heart.

We all have our individual and cultural reasons for eating, and some of them do not benefit our health. Some are for our emotions. We are human, susceptible, and weak sometimes. However, that does not make us anything less than anyone else. Accept your weaknesses. Master your pleasures, and carry on.

It's OK to indulge for whatever reason it may be—a frustrating day or a planned indulgence. But just don't indulge all the time, or out of habit. Know that food cannot and will never replace love and joy, or whatever desires your journal writing is uncovering. Laugh at yourself, smile during your rare indulgences, and balance them with good eating habits the rest of the time.

Always know what, when, where, and why you are eating. Keep writing in your journal to answer those questions. You will love getting to know yourself through writing. There's a good chance your journal will become a special place, a confidant, and a good habit. By means of a good habit—writing—you'll see all the bad habits you've developed, and that's just fine. Because you'll see the facts in print, on the page, that tell you that you can change.

Here's another one of my mistakes. A few months ago after a very healthy dinner, Amy's single-serving pizza and spinach sautéed with a little butter and garlic, I foolishly grabbed the leftover package of Ghirardelli's semi-sweet chocolate chips. I knew as I sat down in front of the TV with the half package of chocolate—6 ounces—that that was a dangerous thing to do. Mindless eating ahead! What I should have done was pour out a small handful in a bowl, a calorically sensible serving size, 2 or 3 tablespoons for about 150 calories. Then I could have harmlessly enjoyed my treat, savoring a few chips at a time. But, alas, no! I grabbed the package and sat down in front of the TV, unable to stop eating them, and incurred a whopping 600-calorie addition to my caloric budget of 2000 for the day.

I also had a much-deserved sleepless night because of the caffeine and sugar in the chocolate. I had simply eaten too much.

The Ghirardelli chocolate chips were delectable—the sensation, the flavor, and the letting go, the devil-may-care fun of it all. I had let down my guard and allowed a purely indulgent pleasure to master me, instead of my mastering it. The next morning I suffered. I was tired and anxious. I also lessened my ability to have a wonderful and productive day because I was on edge. And all this because of a five-minute, out-of-control eating splurge. Darn! Human again.

We all indulge from time to time. No one is a perfect eating, performing, and thinking machine. It's been months since I've overindulged, and it will be months, maybe never, before I again have those chocolate chips in my pantry. *If you can't control your eating of something, like me with chocolate chips, do not have it in your house.*

Usually I am really good, sticking to my good habits, and enjoying my meals and my health. I have kept within two or three pounds of my ideal weight for twelve years. I do not despair over out-of-control indulgences, but every time I avoid an episode of mindless eating I shout "Hallelujah!"

You can do the same. Treat yourself to a play, a good movie, a new video game, fresh flowers, a new book, a CD, or a new hairstyle. Celebrate your power. Celebrate another solid stone laid, or another brushstroke applied in a painterly way. You have moved ahead measurably on your journey toward health and empowerment. Learn to sing with life and be a participator. Most of all, love this journey as you record in your journal one more avoidance of mindless, out-of-control eating . . . and then another . . . and another.

You will learn to love yourself and see your potential through small steps of triumph. Look at yourself in the mirror after such acts of awareness, avoidance, and strength. Look at yourself in exactly the way you would want your mother, father, coach, or teacher to look at you—with appreciation, approval, and acknowledgment. Smile at yourself, and see how beautiful or how handsome you are in your triumph.

Another reason for eating out of control, eating from indulgence, is that you love food and the sheer greedy joy of it. You may consider yourself a gourmand. Others may consider you a glutton. Either way, by your self-indulgent actions, you are choosing guilt, shame, and ill health. You are choosing a racing heart at night, being out of breath after a few steps, sleepless nights, and then, of course, all the diseases that derive from indulgence.

This book is not for those who choose heart disease, obesity, diabetes, and cancer—often the diseases of the self-indulgent. Instead, this book is for those who want to enjoy food and life while feeling good and celebrating their body and their well-being.

For twenty-five hundred years our Western culture has been promoting "civilized eating," the affluent eating and drinking described in T. Colin Campbell's *The China Study* (2005). Campbell addresses many aspects of our diets, including institutional research, disease, and our ability to reverse disease. I highly recommend his book for anyone wanting to understand the powerful message our food industry disseminates and their influence over us all. I also recommend this book for understanding the power of good food.

His research reveals that heart disease, obesity, diabetes, and cancer are diseases of the affluent. Campbell cites the ancient Greek philosophers' predictions that in the distant future, civilization would require more doctors to cure disease and lawyers to litigate land rights to grow cattle and crops for profit. All the meat eating you see causes disease and utilizes too much land. The Greek philosophers were on to something.

Frances Moore Lappé describes in *Diet for a Small Planet* (1991) the wasteful use of land. The American livestock industry requires 20 million tons of soy and vegetable protein to produce 2 million tons of beef. The 18 million tons lost in the process could provide 12 urgently needed grams of protein daily to everyone in the world. "We feed almost half the world's grain to livestock, returning only a fraction in meat—while millions starve. It confounds all logic." Plato surmised that in the future, society would suffer under unnecessary expense and ill health because of its "civilized" eating habits that rely mostly on meat. The land and water needed to subsidize that way of life are enormous, as recorded more recently in Lappé's book. Plato's was a pretty good prediction, wouldn't you say? But even prescient Plato did not foresee our current worldwide starvation as another unintended consequence of our support for an affluent, meat-eating society.

I am, as we all are, influenced by the society in which we live. But it is often empowering to question the status quo.

Let's first question our meat-eating, sick, and litigious society by educating ourselves. I hope this book simplifies the process and inspires you to continue to question the status quo. A while back I thought of titling this book "Just Don't Eat Anything the Government Says Is OK to Eat."

While our government appears to be making good, strong changes—as exemplified by the new dietary pyramid, MyPyramid—my research has led me to believe there still remains some truth to my earlier title. We are all bankrolling a powerful and self-serving food industry that the FDA has neither the staff nor the will to police effectively. While visiting in the hospital a friend suffering from pancreatic cancer, I noticed an informational pamphlet, "The Nutrition You Need Now." The title implies that only when we contract a deadly disease do we need to address healthy eating. A little backward thinking, wouldn't you say? Nestlé subsidized and wrote the pamphlet.

The food industry subsidizes many of the major nutritional studies done in this country. Do you really want Nestlé, the American Meat Institute, Kraft, Coca-Cola, General Mills, the National Dairy Council, and Oscar Mayer, to name a few (see Fuhrman, 1998), telling you what is nutritious and healthy for you to eat? The pamphlet from the hospital shocked me because it showed not one picture of a fruit or a vegetable. It promoted only laboratory-produced substitutes for foods, such as Resource Breeze in a box, Impact in a box, and what looks like Breakfast in a can. This pamphlet stands as an egregious example of the nutritional crisis we have in this country. Our bodies, even the bodies of cancer patients, are sometimes controlled by big, powerful food conglomerates.

I have sympathy for the obese and the sick because they are constantly manipulated by false information. In his *Fasting and Eating for Health* (1998), Dr. Joel Fuhrman writes, "Much of the nutritional information given to the public is misleading. Even food labeling is deceptive." He is referring, for example, to the many different names for sugar, frustrating the reader's ability to decipher a food label to his or her benefit.

Wake up, America, and educate and empower yourselves! Regain your health and your autonomy. Say "no" to fast food, processed food, refined carbohydrates, and false information about proteins. Ask how healthy our animal products are, and how healthy they are for our planet. Say "no" to diseases of the affluent. Say "no" to false research promoted and subsidized by the profit-driven food industry that helps to make us sick. Joel Fuhrman's, Michael Pollan's, David A. Kessler's, John Robbins's and T. Colin Campbell's books all support these facts. And they strongly advocate improving our health by questioning the status quo.

No one is saying that our food industry's intention is to make us sick, but that is the result, done with smooth efficacy. On the June 14, 2009, *60 Minutes*, the mayor of San Francisco said, "We consume lousy food. It is killing us." He was part of a segment where Leslie Stahl interviewed Alice Waters, chef and owner of Berkeley's Chez Panisse Café and a persuasive activist in promoting healthy food production and availability.

Back in the 1960s and 1970s, America and the world experienced an upsurge in population growth. The question of the hour, as climate change is now, was how would we feed the world's population? Mexico and India were running out of food. People were starving, and the world needed answers. We came up with chemicals to ward off pests that endangered our crops, and cheap processed foods were created in the laboratories. Those answers, well intended, relied on quick responses to immediate circumstances, and they backfired. We just didn't look far enough into the future.

The widely used pesticide DDT has been found to be the cancer-causing scourge of the chemical world, and the refining and processing of our foods has removed the very nutritional value that we sought. This is a controversial area, generating many books on all sides. Nevertheless, while the food industry and our government had good intentions, they in fact opened a can of worms.

So why do we eat? Since 1960 we have been influenced if not driven by marketing, false advertising, and the presumption that we have no time. We are what we eat, and the public's health—not just that of the affluent—has been harmed by time misuse, leading to stress and a serious lack of autonomous power. We're moving too fast, without thought or awareness. Our rushed efforts lack efficacy. Also, the fashion is to prize hurried and stressed lifestyles; we look and feel busy, so we think we must be important. The result is a gross misuse of our time. The result is our yielding to unhealthy, outside pressure to *be* somebody—but who or what kind of person? To be an automaton, a plaything of popular culture, a performing machine removed from nature and spirit? To be a populace fast becoming an inhuman mass of destructive energy?

But you can fight your own destructive energy by becoming a more conscious being, which means knowing yourself. Without this awakening, writes Eckhart Tolle in *The Power of Now*, the human species will continue to be "dangerously insane and very sick."

Slow down and satisfy yourself by being aware and in control of your life and your health. Plan your day, including what you will eat, and know yourself. Choose your foods wisely, and master your indulgences with self-knowledge and self-acceptance. I just lost a good friend to cancer. I wanted to assuage my sadness, but not incur guilt and remorse. So I prepared a grand yet healthy meal of baked chicken, mashed potatoes, and green beans. Good comfort food.

Slow down and get to know yourself by writing in your journal. Record on a daily basis what, when, where, and why you eat, the four Ws. Be present and aware of your surroundings, all that is spoken and all that you see. Yesterday on my morning walk with Chaps, my Jack Russell terrier, I couldn't help but see the abundance in nature. Little white blossoms in the midst of the dry, fall leaves. Then I thought of the migrating birds and the optimism they signify in their grueling yearly migration. Record your reactions, your perceptions, your disappointments, and all your joys. Conjure "an attitude of gratitude," as author and personality Maya Angelou says she does every day. Write in detail, because details you set down on the page show you just who you are. Read your entries back to yourself. In time, you may decide to read to others what you have written. Perhaps you might want to share them in a book club geared for health.

Converse with yourself. While acknowledging your triumphs, speak to yourself in the mirror with praise and kind words. Today I said to the reflection in the mirror, "You look pretty good!" Yesterday I said, "What are you going to do with that hair?" And I laughed. Dance in front of the mirror; check yourself out. Strut, and if you don't see what you want to see, imagine!

Choose conscious living. Feel for and with others. I got a call from Franci, whom I love. She and her husband, eighteen-month-old Cash, and Fuggles, their German wirehaired pointer, just lost their other most wonderful dog, Firkin. I cried and recorded how I felt while sharing her grief. I was grateful for her friendship, grateful that I could offer some solace in a phone call, and glad that I was so alive and conscious that I could feel her grief.

Don't let busy times and the food industry control your life. Take control of your life by being aware and knowing yourself. Observe this beautiful planet, and accept that bad things happen. Most of all, celebrate life by being the nurturing caregiver your body needs. After all, it is your precious body and your very valuable life. Live it well!

CHAPTER FIVE

Know Your Body

Creating a functional life is much easier when you have a functional body. Know your body. Listen to your body. Appreciate your body. According to Paul McKenna, writing in *I Can Make You Thin*, "You've got to make friends with the body you have in order to get the body you want." Be clear about your body image. Do you think of yourself as fat or thin? If you want to be thin, you must think like a thin person.

Thinking like a thin person involves self-respect, and it requires comfort with your body. Have you ever noticed a person who is comfortable with herself or himself? How they exude composure and ease, a kind of grace? I was visiting friends I hadn't seen in a very long time. We live all over the

United States and had not been together in years. After a great weekend as things were winding down, I asked my friend Linda, "Why does it feel so good to be around Helen?"

"Because Helen is so comfortable in her own skin," Linda said. I wanted to know how she got that way. I wanted to be like her—composed, confident without conceit, alert and interested, seeming to have all the time in the world to listen. Helen is an accomplished woman with a career. She's also a good mother. She has been married to the same man for about forty years. She is smart, fun, and interesting. What made her like this? I don't know for sure, but I'll bet her parents supported and encouraged her. I am guessing, too, that she knows herself and likes herself. Isn't that what this is all about? Knowing and liking ourselves?

If you want to be comfortable in your own skin and have the will to care for yourself like the precious gift you are, first make friends with yourself. Make friends with your body.

Along with making friends with yourself, understand the importance of exercise and movement. I love to walk—not a meandering, strolling walk, but an energetic and uplifting walk. FitTV has great exercise classes and yoga. I particularly like to do the *Namaste* yoga class. I have followed *Sports Illustrated*'s video "Super Shape-Up Program" since 1986. I like "Stretch and Strengthen" with Elle MacPherson. You can get these videos online for about a $1.50 per video, and you can't beat that! Elle says in the beginning of the video, "I think exercise should be something that is a pleasure to do." Boy, do I agree! Why do something that you hate to do, something that eventually you will stop doing?

Get in the groove of moving your body to your pleasure. So many activities encourage friendship with your body. I turn on some hot music and dance when I clean up after dinner. I call it my dancing-in-the-kitchen music. I like to stretch a lot because it seems to enliven my whole being. Even when reading, I like to get up and stretch or take a walk for a break. I never worry about parking close to my destination; the little walk will do me good. Every little movement is better than no movement. I love my walks with Chaps. I walk two miles every day. I call it my morning coffee because it does the same as a cup of coffee; it revs up the start of my day. Moving enlivens you, sharpens you, and keeps you awake, both physically and consciously to yourself and to your always fascinating surroundings, no matter where you live.

As to being awake, conscious, and aware, slow down in order to ease your everyday performance—brushing and flossing your teeth, preparing breakfast, driving alertly to work, dropping off the kids at school or getting on the bus to school, and making a clear plan for the day, including what you will eat and how you will get exercise. Methodical, clear, and aware use of time produces efficacy—a better product, a better day, and a better you. It eliminates stress and enables good planning. And I don't know anything that can be accomplished without a plan. "Planned eating can recondition your behavior," writes David A. Kessler in *The End of Overeating*. Planning your day establishes good habits and eliminates the bad. Think about it. How often do you grab something to eat that is bad for your body because you didn't have a plan? Often, I bet. I used to do it, too.

Along with thinking like a thin and confident person, stretching and exercising, and slowing down and planning, listen to your body. Your body always tells you what it needs, though you may not have been listening. Learn the difference between cravings and body needs. A craving is emotionally based, but a body need is physically based. Your body is like the universe; it wants what's best for you. For example, once in a while I want meat, or broccoli, or a banana. My body tells me it wants protein, or the vitamins and minerals in the broccoli or the banana. Sometimes I crave chocolate or a beer. Now I realize that this is a craving caused by low blood sugar or by sadness. Know the difference. Sadness does not disappear because you've ingested chocolate or drunk a beer, and low blood sugar can easily and more efficaciously be cured with a piece of fruit, a tablespoon of peanut butter, a slice of cheese, or a cup of bouillon.

First, let's recognize that every synapse, neuron, neurotransmitter, atom, and cell in your muscles, bones, brain, eyes, teeth, hair, and skin need vitamins, and macro- and micronutrients to function. For example, do you know that the liver cleanses the blood of dangerous toxins we ingest every day from food, pollution, and chemicals? The liver also helps to metabolize our food, produces clotting factors, and promotes wound healing; it's even involved in immune function. That's a lot of hard work, yet it's just one organ in our miraculous body.

Again, creating a functional life is much easier with a functional body. Your body is your only vehicle through this life. Witness how it carries you along on your magical journey of pure potential. Think how incredible your sole means of transportation through life, your workhorse of a body, is! It breathes for you, pumps blood for you, and it enables thinking, feeling, planning, acting, and creating. So, treat your vehicle, your body, well, and cherish it.

Let's look at how to do that. Immediately let's figure your approximate healthy weight. Here is the equation. If you are a female, for every inch in height over 5 feet, add 5 pounds to 100 pounds. I am 5 feet 5 inches tall, and a female, so my desired weight is 125 pounds, or 100 plus 5 x 5 = 125 pounds.

If you are a male, we change the equation a little by starting at 5 feet but 106 pounds; then add 6 pounds per inch to 106 pounds over 5 feet. So, if you are a male and you are 6 feet tall, your ideal weight will be 178 pounds, or 106 pounds plus 6 x 12 = 178.

Always remember just how smart your body is and how much it wants to help you. When you are near your goal weight and your body wants to weigh 5 or 10 pounds more or less than your "ideal" weight of, say, 178, the reason is that those few pounds' difference signifies your individual ideal weight. You cannot just randomly pick a weight and think that you can maintain it healthfully. Your weight must fit your body's type and needs.

Paul McKenna writes in *I Can Make You Thin* that our bodies contain a natural blueprint for optimal health. I weigh 125 pounds, and it is easy to maintain this weight. I really feel good and thin at 122 pounds, but that weight is difficult to maintain, so I go with what my body dictates.

Now that you know your approximate healthy weight, here is how body knowledge will help you reach and maintain that weight. One, by our choice of foods we can ease digestion of what we eat. Two, the consequence of that ease can, in turn, strengthen our metabolism. Our bodies spend a vast amount of energy digesting food. Digestion begins in our mouth and travels through the many digestive organs, such as our esophagus, our stomach, our liver, our kidneys, our pancreas, our small intestine, and our large intestine. Quite a journey, wouldn't you say? It is a complex and miraculous process. We can choose poorly, making it difficult and debilitating for our bodies to digest food, or we can ease the process and, in turn, enable our energy and health. Educated, healthful choices help our bodies function efficiently.

The easiest foods to digest are fruits and vegetables. The hardest to digest are animal proteins and fats. Nina Simonds, in *Spoonful of Ginger*, tells us that the Chinese prefer eggs, fish, and poultry because they are the easiest of the animal proteins to digest. To this ancient food culture, pork remains neutral while beef and lamb are left for the winter months because of their warming features. The Chinese also know that eating cruciferous vegetables such as cauliflower and broccoli with beef and lamb aids in the digestion of these heavy, warming meats.

You could simplify the algorithm and eat mostly fruits and vegetables but very little protein and fat. Another good reason to enable your body to digest food more easily is that in eating plant foods, you will be able to eat more without gaining weight and, consequently, build your metabolism. In *The China Study*, Campbell tells us that although the Chinese calorie intake is higher than ours, they have an average of 20 percent less body weight. *Your metabolism, like your brain or your muscles, needs exercise to become stronger.* The following figure shows digestive degrees of difficulty in our food choices, with the easiest on top.

Fruits
Vegetables
Grains and flours
Legumes
Nuts and seeds
Dairy, eggs, fish, and all flesh foods

Keep this figure in your mind at all times, as handy as your calorie counter, in order to lose weight or maintain your weight, and to instill energy and health. *Eat more of what is easy to digest and less of what is difficult to digest.* You can make that choice.

Another way to ease digestion is food combining. Dr. Herbert Shelton discovered that certain combinations of food create havoc in our digestive system, leading to the prolific use of stomach pain relievers such as antacids. The worst food combination is protein followed by fruit. Picture a video of your digestive system and watch the slowest food to digest, meat, enter your system, first the mouth, and down to the stomach. Follow this dense, sinewy, and fat-laden food along the arduous digestive path.

Now see fruit, the fastest and easiest food to digest, enter right after the meat. The fruit being held up by the meat says, "Hey, I can't get through! I'm stuck on top of this slowpoke meat! Help!" And there, stuck in your digestive tract, the fruit starts to ferment, stagnate, and cause the familiar discomforts of gas, indigestion, and heartburn. As your body has to deal with this dysfunction, your energy is sapped and your resolve to lose weight vanishes because you feel lousy.

Another bad food combination we Americans live on is starch and protein. My goodness, no wonder we are all sick and living on diet soda or some other caffeine source to stimulate energy. Again, this combination is difficult to process. The body needs lots of energy to digest starch and protein. Ever been sleepy after a meal of eggs and bacon and toast? My dad used to say after a big breakfast like that, "Well, that will put me right back to sleep." Have you gone out to lunch only to feel tired and listless an hour after eating? It's your dysfunctional food combining. Those heavy meat sandwiches leave you tired and broke every time. Back to the Chinese, whom I admire so much for their knowledge of food and its effects on our bodies: they don't eat sandwiches laden with fatty, salty meats and cheeses. Instead, they combine heavy meats with vegetables.

If you want to know more about food combining, I highly recommend reading Shelton's book. But here I can suggest that you be aware of debilitating combinations. Either avoid them, or lessen their effects with food knowledge. If you insist on eating bad food combinations on a daily basis, you will sabotage your weight loss or maintenance, and you will sap your energy. Also, your metabolism will suffer. You don't want to wear it down; you want to build it up!

Beef, lamb, and pork are the densest meats/proteins to digest. Next come chicken, fish, eggs, and cheeses. Thus, you want to combine eggs, fish, or cheese with starches, not heavy meats. One of my favorite dinners is fish, potatoes, and a salad or a vegetable. If I have steak or pork, I eat it with a vegetable, not a starch. Also, I eat animal protein rarely—about once a week at the most.

Campbell says we need about 10 percent of our daily food intake to be protein, and for me that's about 150 to 200 calories a day, or 10 percent of 1500 to 2000 calories a day. Two hundred calories is 4 ounces of lean flesh food a day. Don't forget that we ingest protein in many other sources, such as beans, nuts, fruits, and vegetables, so every day we get some protein. Most important, back to fruit, I eat my fruit in the morning. "Breakfast" really means you are breaking the fast of abstaining from food from dinner to breakfast, and a fast, whether short or long, should be broken by eating small amounts of fruit, the easiest food to digest.

Fruit is my favorite food. As with vegetables, the variety of fruits makes them the greatest of all foods. So many luscious, succulent, sweet, and satisfying choices of fruits. So many colors, sizes, and textures. So many nutrients and vitamins packed in such a precious, life-serving treat. Yum! And fruit is so forgiving to our overworked digestive system. Think of pineapple, mango, papaya, pomegranate, orange, lemon, lime, cantaloupe, honeydew, watermelon, grapes, apples—so many kinds! Bananas, pears, kiwi, raspberries, blueberries, blackberries, plums, nectarines, peaches, kumquats, tomatoes, avocados—yes, they are fruits—oh, so many. Go out and start trying them all. Go to your local farmers market to find out what's in season, and always buy organic because the flavor is so much better! Yum, again!

So, what can we all eat the most of while losing weight and maintaining our weight? Fruits and vegetables, our bodies' very best friends. And what foods put weight on the fastest? Heavy, hard-to-digest, poorly combined, glopped-up foods like bacon cheeseburgers, sandwiches piled high with various meats and cheeses, meatball sandwiches, and that good ol' American breakfast—all bad food combinations. Ugh! Have I mentioned sweet, gooey desserts?

Let's take a look at sweet goo and glop by trying a little visualization, a brain retraining trick. Picture your ice cream as hydrogenated fat, the kind in a can of Crisco, a large scoop of pure lard. Picture that chocolate brownie as a large, creamy dog turd. Picture cookies as chewy worms all curled together. Your brain, and I cannot emphasize this enough, is a powerful tool, and it can help you in many ways to lose weight. Try these tricks because they work. Paul McKenna explains them well in his book *I Can Make You Thin*. I've been using these visualization tricks for years.

Doing these mind-altering exercises while knowing how damaging sweets and sugar are to your health and emotional welfare can help kill your desire for these foods and keep you vigilant, on guard against temptation. Nothing is more damaging and addicting than sugar. That is why I call it goo and glop. William Dufty, in *Sugar Blues*, writes, "Through war and peace, depression and prosperity, drought and flood, sugar consumption has risen steadily. It is doubtful there has ever been a more drastic challenge to the human body in the entire history of man."

Goo and glop, does that sound good to you? Of course not. This is how I see our typical American diet. While so many of us are salivating over glopped-up foods like multisensory hamburgers piled high with many varied taste sensations such as mushrooms, cheese, bacon, onions, pickles, and condiments; plates heaped with nachos, cheese, meat, sour cream, tomato salsa, and God knows what else; and desserts like caramel, fudge, pecan, peanut butter sundaes, I see it all as goo and glop. I no longer have a desire for this gloppy food. In fact, I find it disgusting. You can train your brain to change how you look at food.

If you must have sweets, have them once in a while—not daily, not even weekly if you can help it—and have them in small and satisfying amounts. Because the calories in sweets are so high and add up so quickly, when you must have that giant cookie or that piece of pie, have it for your meal. You will have spent 500 to 1000 calories, wasted your money, and you will get very little back for those expenditures of calories and cash. You will get no nutrition, no vitamins, and no lasting energy, but you will get a tired, blah feeling laced with shame, guilt, and a lowered resolve to care for yourself. Sugar is addictive: the more you eat, the more you want.

Notice this truth about your body. Write in your journal just how you feel after eating sweets. Then, the next day, recognize how you think you want another helping of something sweet, and then another. Sweets are a no-win game. Read William Dufty's *Sugar Blues*, the deeply researched classic on sugar and its devastating effects on our health.

Eat instead for energy and health. Eat good food to feel good. Do not eat bad food, gloppy food, gooey food, refined and processed food, heavy and hard-to-digest food, because you will feel bad. Use herbs and spices to your healthy advantage. Ginger, cayenne, turmeric, garlic, dill, thyme, rosemary, mint, and parsley all help digestion. Remember Confucius's words of close self-awareness, "I must have ginger in my food for my digestion." You, too, can practice being aware of which foods make your body digest well and which do not. Here's a cleansing drink that includes ginger: put a cup of apple or orange juice in a blender, add a tablespoon of lemon juice, a pinch of cayenne pepper, a handful of chopped parsley, a teaspoon or more of fresh chopped ginger, add a cut-up frozen banana, and blend till nice and frothy. It's yummy and so good for you!

Fasting is also good for our body. Our body exhausts itself by digesting bad food, and that exhaustion is exacerbated by the bad food combinations of the American diet. Give it a rest and fast for health and rejuvenation, but only under clinical supervision. Joel Furhman's book, *Fasting and Eating for Health*, explains the benefits. He fasted at the same place I fasted in the 1970s, Dr. Shelton's Health School, in San Antonio. What a learning experience we all had, with daily lectures on food and our digestive system. Furhman went on to become a doctor; his book explores our food industry, medical science, and eating and fasting for health. Whether you choose to fast—and it must be done under supervision, as I said—or whether you decide to cleanse as well as you can, these practices are very good for your system.

Dr. Gillian McKeith's *You Are What You Eat* gives some great suggestions for how to cleanse your digestive tract. I use Trace Minerals' Complete Cleansing and Anti-Toxin System Part 2 on a daily basis. I just add it to my morning milkshake. The cleaner your pipes, the easier for digestion to take place and the more energy and health you will have. Our work-horse of a body must absorb nutrients and vitamins as the food travels through our long, winding digestive system. Isn't it simple logic that if all those pipes and avenues are clean, the process of absorption is simplified? Make it easy for your body to be healthy.

Be kind to yourself, and get to know your body. Respect your body, and thank your body every day by eating good, nutritious meals that are easy to digest. Learn to love the body given to you, a precious gift. Accept your body, and be comfortable in your own skin. That alone will take off 10 pounds. You know how? Because when you are proud of and grateful for your body, it will show in your carriage and your demeanor. You will look better to others because you will stand taller and walk with grace and confidence. You will show that you are beginning to love yourself and that you are willing to share yourself with others, always respectful of your chosen boundaries. *Let your body say to the world, "Look at me, I love myself, and I invite you to do the same!"*

CHAPTER SIX

Good Foods Tell the Truth

I wonder why in India, in China, in Europe, and throughout the world—really, everywhere except in the United States—people understand the rejuvenating and medicinal qualities of food, herbs, and spices. Just turn to any page in *A Spoonful of Ginger* and find references to the medicinal qualities of everything from mushrooms, carrots, and cabbage to star anise, garlic, and ginger. A sample: "Our immune system is the key to health and longevity and there are many factors that throw off our yin/yang balance. When this happens, traditional Chinese medicine often uses herbal tonics and food to help restore the balance."

Here's another: "In Europe peppermint has been used medicinally for thousands of years." And, "Tangerine and orange peel are reputed to warm the body, clear any congested energy channels, and help regulate energy flow." I asked a local Indian restaurant owner if it was true that most Indians grow up understanding that turmeric aids digestion and that cayenne can help cleanse our system. Yes, they do, he said. I'll repeat the Italian adage, "It's better to pay the grocer than the doctor." The rest of the world knows the health properties and the values of good, wholesome foods. In the United States, however, we manipulate, process, and refine food with the end result being a degraded, valueless product in a cute box.

Isn't it more fun and certainly more beneficial to eat whole food, real food, high-quality good food that hasn't been toyed with? Isn't it empowering to understand the healing qualities of real food so that you can avoid being a puppet of our food industry, serving its profits over your health? Well, you can do that, starting right now. We are going on a food discovery.

There are good foods and bad foods. Good foods serve you, and bad foods make you sick. *Good foods tell the truth.* A banana is a banana, an orange an orange, an apple an apple, a green pepper a green pepper, and a tomato a tomato. Good foods are clean and unadulterated, without processing, fixing, or chemicals—just pure, nutritional, sweet goodness. Good foods do not need flavor additives. Good foods strengthen our energies, awaken us to variety, and satisfy our palates. Educate yourself about what you are eating. Go to the reference list at the back of this book and start reading. Do not let yourself be fooled into eating fake food. Eat real food that your body knows how to handle. Doesn't your body—don't you—deserve it?

After all, we live in an organic body. We come from the earth. We are not bioengineered, and we are not technologically or chemically produced. We are pure organic physiology warranting pure organic sustenance, sustenance supporting our life and our health. All life is purely organic, coming from the earth, and some would say from God. Who would want to mess with that?

Here is a quick list of bad foods: any food that is refined, processed, or adulterated in any way. That would be most of the foods in the central aisles of your local grocery-store chain. In *Eat This, Not That*, authors Zinczenko and Goulding make a great suggestion: shop on the outskirts of the store in produce, organic, vegetarian, fish, poultry, and dairy. These food sections are located around the periphery of the grocery store. Why? Because the store's profit margin on these foods is narrower. Instead, the store wants you to see and head for boxed, prepared convenience foods, sugared cereals, cookies, chips, and soft drinks—the products that make the most money for the store, and for several good reasons—one of which is longer shelf life. Another quick trick to recognizing these manipulated foods is to look at the ingredient list. If that list is more than a few quick lines, like a paragraph, most likely the product is refined to the hilt with many food additives.

Simply put, bad foods are not from the ground or a tree or a plant. Bad foods come from laboratories, manufacturing plants, and bioengineering. Again, from *Sugar Blues*: "Once the grain is pulverized, it will not sprout, it cannot reproduce itself." You see, it is a dead food; its life force has been thwarted and disabled. All plants and animals have a life force, an energy, and even a spirit. The more live, energy-filled food we eat, the better we feel, spirit feeding spirit. Bad foods are dead, without spirit, and deaden our spirits. Judith Orloff, assistant clinical professor of psychiatry at UCLA explains in *Positive Energy*:

POSITIVE-ENERGY FOODS (ALIVE FOODS): radiate a glow, are fragrant, filling, energizing, organic, chemical and preservative-free. They won't give you the impulse to overeat.

NEGATIVE-ENERGY FOODS (DEAD FOODS): Appear limp or tired, lack fragrance, are unsatisfying, sap energy or add none, contain preservatives and chemicals or are enriched; make you bloated, or ill: stimulate overeating and sugar/carbohydrate binges.

So what about meats? Well, there are good flesh foods and bad flesh foods. Our industrial food industry has been abusing animals for a long time now, and many of us will not buy factory-farmed animal products. These factory-farmed animals contain antibiotics and hormones, which are bad for us. The antibiotics are needed to stem the disease caused by overcrowding, and the hormones are used to ensure speedy, though unhealthful growth.

Good meats are clean—meaning free of drugs—and the living animals are handled in a friendly manner. Chickens are not raised in filthy, caged conditions. Pigs are allowed to roam and are not crated, which causes distress and fear. It is just plain cruel and inhumane. Beef cattle are allowed to graze, as opposed to being fed in overcrowded feedlots and helplessly standing in their own feces. Observing our food industry and factory farming system would make the farmer of yesteryear weep with shame. An example of this shame can be seen in the 2008 film *Food Inc.*, where an industrial chicken farmer sheds tears of frustration and shame as she sweeps up the dead chickens left behind and describes the ones that can't walk due to their enlarged breasts grown for our consumption.

Eating these "dis-spirited" products containing no good energy can only wreak havoc on our bodies and our spirits. Michael Pollan writes in *The Omnivore's Dilemma*:

> A tension has always existed between the capitalist imperative to maximize efficiency at any cost and the moral imperatives of culture, which historically have served as a counterweight to the moral blindness of the market. This is another example of the cultural contradictions of capitalism—the tendency over time for the economic impulse to erode

the moral underpinnings of society. Mercy toward
the animals in our care is one such casualty.

The industrial animal factory offers a nightmarish glimpse of what capitalism is capable of in
the absence of any moral or regulatory constraint
whatsoever.

If we make a little effort and educate ourselves, good, clean
proteins are available to us all. Try Whole Foods Market if
you have one near you. I drive sixty miles to my nearest one
just to ensure that I am not supporting torture. The Internet
is also a good source of humanely raised products. Just do an
Internet search for "organic," or go to eatwellguide.org or eat-
wild.com. You can also search the Internet for places in your
state that sell local products.

Our nation is improving its treatment of processed animals. On July 13, 2009, U.S. Rep. Louise Slaughter (D.-N.Y.)
said, "I feel sorry for people who only have been able to eat
factory-raised animals." As a microbiologist and chairwoman
of the Rules Committee, Rep. Slaughter was holding a hearing on antimicrobial animal drugs. This hearing is available

on C-SPAN's Web site. I recommend it for anyone concerned about the overuse of drugs in animal farming.

Also read the "Pig Farmer" chapter in *Food Revolution: How Your Diet Can Help Save Your Life and the World*, by John Robbins. In this beautiful story of conscious reckoning and change, a hog farmer sells his farm after years of misery and shame. As described here, factory farming is reminiscent of Auschwitz. The hog farmer in Robbins's account moves to another state, works closely with 4-H, and opens a pig-petting farm. What a blessed man!

Sugar is another killer food. Sugar can keep you depressed, make you tired and listless, and is strongly addictive. The more you eat, the more you want. Killing your palate and your range of tastes, sugar is disguised under numerous pseudonyms such as sucrose, high fructose, high-fructose corn syrup (HFCS), dextrose, glucose, lactose, malt, maltodextrin, maltose, and treacle. This killer of a food product is in just about every processed food—most cereals, boxed meals, canned soups, refined foods, packaged breads and rolls, convenience foods, and most frozen foods, such as pizza and frozen dinners. Just about everything in the center of your grocery store, including so-called power drinks, contains sugar. We have doubled our consumption of sugar since 1983, so watch out! Eat only whole-grain products. Eat clean foods that have not been altered with chemicals and sugar, and eat healthy animal products for a healthier you.

Bad foods are laden with chemicals and drugs. As I said before, if the label on a particular food item—bread or cereal, frozen pizza or a can of soup—is more than a couple lines long and has many long, undecipherable words, the item contains things you really don't want to ingest.

Look to other cultures. They eat real foods that come from pastures, trees, and plants. Don't be fooled by degraded ethnic food that has been changed to please an American palate conditioned to salt, fat, and sugar. Kessler writes in *The End of Overeating*, "Asian food has become hugely popular in the United States—but what we're eating here is not what has traditionally been eaten across the Pacific." Look at real Chinese and Indian food, clean sushi, and Japanese food. Look at how Asians eat in Dr. Campbell's *The China Study*. They consume less protein and more fresh vegetables. They certainly do not eat our grocery store "Asian" that is tainted with food coloring and MSG to enhance flavor.

Learn about how food is prepared healthfully and tastefully by reading good cookbooks, a few of which are referenced at the back of this book. Always remember: *bad foods lie*, sometimes appearing to be simple good food. Recognize that to be fat free, sugar free, and salt free, something else has replaced these items, something that is most likely mysterious and questionable. What do the manufacturers add to make them taste like the fat, sugar, and salt they are removing? Chemicals. Educate yourself, day by day. Don't be fooled by tricky phrases and slick packaging. You will feel empowered and in control of your life and your health, a great way to feel.

I just went out to get something to eat because my larder was empty and I have an evening meeting. Very unusual for me not to have something healthy and yummy on hand. So I ran over to a fresh market here in town and picked up a "Deluxe Chicken Caesar Salad." I thought salad might be the least offensive prepared lunch. But here is the ingredient list I copied off the label on the plastic container:

Ingredients: lettuce, chicken, 15% added solution water, seasoning (salt, sodium phosphate, maltodextrin, hydrolyzed corn gluten, torula yeast, soy flour, rice extractive), croutons (enriched bromated flour, wheat and malted barley flour, niacin, reduced iron, thiamine mononitrate, riboflavin, potassium bromate), water, natural sourdough flavor (starch, natural flavors, vegetable shortening, lecithin), yeast salt, dough conditioner (wheat flour, diacetyl, esters of mono & diglycerides, soy lecithin, potassium, bromate, soybean oil, l-cysteine, boric acid, fungal amylase), vegetable oil, whole wheat, rye, sesame, sunflower seeds, wheat germ, molasses, brown sugar, salt, soy oil, barley, buckwheat, corn, rice flours, millet, triticale, rice meal, ascorbic acid, olive oil, red and black pepper, unsalted butter, parmesan cheese, dressing (egg yolk, salt, sugar, spices, anchovies, citric acid, garlic, lemon juice concentrate, monosodium glutamate, xanthan gum, maltodextrin, onion, polysorbate 60, sodium benzoate, natural flavors, molasses, caramel color,

calcium sodium EDTA, tamarind, disodium ino-
sinate, disodium guanylate).

I was very hungry, but did I want to eat this? As my friend
Rollin said, "Don't eat anything you can't pronounce!" Just
look at the various additives: hydrolyzed corn gluten, diacetyl,
fungal amylase, esters of mono & diglycerides, triticale, maltodextrin, sodium phosphate, sodium benzoate, and monosodium glutamate. Amazing! Are we machines made to process
chemicals? *Bad foods lie.* I expected chicken, lettuce, croutons
made of bread, grated cheese, and dressing. Instead, I got chemicals. But why do they need all these additives to make a simple
chicken and lettuce salad? Why so many chemicals and flavorings? For one thing, flavorings make factory-farmed chicken
taste like chicken because in reality it tastes like nothing.

An argument is going on throughout the world against U.S.
bioengineered food products. Some say these scientifically con-
ceived food products might harm the environment by killing
off butterflies and contaminating clean organic crops, even
harming our health. The European Union has banned the
use of antibiotics on animals, and has fought against our food

industry products, including paying a "150-million-dollar-a-year tariff rather than allow U.S. beef to cross their borders." Independent scientists find "that some hormones added to U.S. meat are complete carcinogens capable of causing cancer" (John Robbins, *Food Revolution*). "Since 1998 the European Union commission has not approved any applications for farming gene-altered crops" (*New York Times*, Nov. 6, 2008).

Do we want to feed our organic bodies with chemically and bioengineered food products? Do we want to support contaminating our earth with these products? And why is the U.S. pushing these products down the throats of the rest of the world? Profit over health. Think about what you do to your body every day. Be informed and be aware. And most important, have fun with and enjoy the gifts of the earth—clean, organic, humanely raised food products that raise your health and your spirit!

FOOD: A CLOSER LOOK

Let's take a more detailed look at food, dividing it into six groups:

1. Fruits
2. Vegetables
3. Grains
4. Legumes
5. Nuts and seeds
6. Dairy, eggs, fish, and meats

In the following diagram you can see that the easiest foods to digest and what we want the most of are on top, and the most difficult to digest or the hardest foods on our bodies are on the bottom:

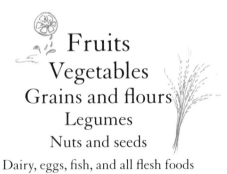

Fruits
Vegetables
Grains and flours
Legumes
Nuts and seeds
Dairy, eggs, fish, and all flesh foods

The first two groups, fruits and vegetables, contain everything we need to survive and be healthy. They are rich in vitamins, minerals, and fiber, plus protein.

FRUITS

∞ Oranges, lemons, tangerines, limes, grapefruit, bananas,
papayas, pineapples, mangoes, guavas, apples (so many: Gala,
Jonathan, Macintosh, Granny Smith, Golden Delicious, Fuji,
and Red Delicious), pears (Bartlett and Bosc), grapes (red
and green), watermelons, cantaloupes, honeydews, peaches,
plums, nectarines, apricots, cherries, blueberries, raspberries,
gooseberries, strawberries, golden raspberries, blackberries,
persimmons, cranberries, star anise, pomegranates, kiwis,
tomatoes, avocados. ∞

A bountiful, luscious cornucopia of sweet succulence! And besides the beauty of the fruit on your plate, consider its glistening sweetness. You can eat all you want. This food group is pure, indulgent joy!

VEGETABLES

❧ Red peppers, green peppers, winter squash, summer squash, acorn squash, potatoes (Yukon, russet, and red), carrots, corn, eggplant, turnips, parsnips, rutabagas, onions, artichokes, greens (turnip, collards, dandelion, kale, Swiss chard, parsley, mustard, and spinach), lettuces (arugula, romaine, red leaf, leaf lettuce, escarole, frisee, endive, and radicchio), asparagus, spring onion, cabbage (Napa, bok choy, savoy, white, and red), hot peppers (Poblano, Jalapeno, Serrano, Habanero), jimica, cucumbers, radishes, celery, broccoli, Brussels sprouts, cauliflower, okra, sweet potatoes, yams, beets, lima beans, green beans, peas, ginger root, garlic, and vegetable oils (olive oil, canola oil, and sunflower oil). ∾

GRAINS AND FLOURS

∾ Barley and buckwheat, cornmeal, corn flour, corn grits as hominy, grits, polenta, millet, quinoa, oats, rice (brown and white), rice bran, rye flour, soy flour, wheat berries, cracked wheat, rolled wheat, wheat bulgar, wheat flour, wheat bran (the outside fiber), wheat germ (the center of the grain), and pasta. ∾

Next come legumes, among the earliest crops cultivated by man. Even in biblical times their nutritional value was known (see *Diet for a Small Planet*).

LEGUMES

∽ Black beans, kidney beans, navy beans, black-eyed peas, fava beans, cannellini, garbanzo, great northern beans, lentils (French, red, and yellow), mung bean, peas, lima beans, split peas, pinto beans, red beans, soybeans (some fermented, as in miso; soybean cake mixed with grains such as tempeh; or soy curd known as tofu), soy milk. ∽

These carbohydrates: grains, flours, and legumes when closest to their natural state and with the least amount of processing, are valuable sources not only of vitamins, minerals, and proteins, but also of fiber—loads of it! Fiber is key to digestion. So, along with fruits and vegetables these grain and pod sources of foods contribute greatly to our energy and our healthy digestion if they are eaten in the correct combinations. We don't want to eat grains and legumes with heavy, dense flesh foods. These food groups are where we get our hot cereals, healthy breads and pastas, hearty soups and salads, and rice dishes. All to be enjoyed ideally without flesh foods, especially the densest of meats, beef, lamb, and pork.

NUTS AND SEEDS

All of the following contain approximately 7 to 9 grams of protein and 150 to 250 calories per half cup. Nuts are a good alternative to animal-based proteins. T. Colin Campbell, in *The China Study*, suggests the less animal-based proteins we eat, the better our health. Our government recommends 5½ ounces of protein per day and recommends that we vary our protein sources. As a nation we eat too much meat, so try other proteins such as nuts to complement your daily nutrition.

❧ Almonds, Brazil nuts, walnuts (black or English), cashews, chestnuts, coconuts, hazelnuts, macadamias, peanuts, pecans, pine nuts, pistachios, pumpkin seeds, sesame seeds, sunflower seeds. ❧

Use nuts or seeds in pastas and stir fries without meat. Use them in rice dishes or in salads. Nuts and seeds are also good as a quick meal or a snack. I like to have nuts available while traveling as a great alternative to fast foods. Nuts are high in protein, fat, calcium, phosphorus, potassium, and energy.

DAIRY, EGGS, FISH, AND MEATS

∾ Milk, butter, cheese (goat, sheep, and cow), cottage cheese, cream, sour cream, ice cream, yogurt, eggs, fish and shellfish, poultry and meats (beef, pork, and lamb). ∾

The animals in this group are sentient, meaning they have a brain stem attached to their nervous system, enabling their sensation and realization of pain and, some say, suffering. Be conscious, conscientious, present, and even grateful in your consumption of these feeling animals. Try to avoid supporting cruel food-industry practices such as crating, caging, and overcrowding. These abuses lead to an unhealthy product that in turn leads to an unhealthy you.

Be aware of and celebrate a world of healthy food choices. The less animal product any person eats, the healthier that person will be. In *The China Study*, the largest nutritional study ever done, according to the *New York Times*, T. Colin Campbell shows that "Nutrition can reverse disease, even genetic disease." The nutrition Campbell writes about begins with lowering our consumption of animal products. He claims that they are the underlying cause of the diseases of the affluent. It's not the product so much as the quantity: we in America eat too much meat.

Just think of the power of food! Good food has power for us, and bad food has power against us. *You make the choice of your physiological future each time you sit down to a meal.*

MENUS AND RECIPES

If you like to eat a lot of food, as I do, here's how. Remember that the more good food you eat in easy-to-digest combinations, the stronger your metabolism will be. Plus, isn't it fun to eat? You may wonder why I don't write these dinners out in traditional recipe form. In order to be healthy, you must learn to prepare your own food to your own taste. So if you don't know how much to add of an ingredient—say, sea salt or Dijon mustard—just add a little and taste; need a little more, add a little more and taste again, until you get it right. Add and taste, add and taste. Never just guess and dump in a whole lot of one flavor. So let me share some of my menus and recipes below:

SAUTÉED FISH, POTATOES WITH DILL, AND SALAD

Buy fish fresh. I always get excellent fish at Whole Foods, and I freeze it at home in individual 4- to 6-ounce serving sizes. Sauté your seasoned fish in a little butter and olive oil. I season with fresh cracked pepper and sea salt. Do not overcook fish. It must be moist and succulent; watch it carefully! A good rule of thumb for cooking fish is five minutes per inch of thickness. Boil small red potatoes, drain, and add a little butter and fresh dill. Add a salad of mixed greens, garlic, olive oil, and Parmigiano Reggiano. Get the real Parmigiano Reggiano, not the tasteless, plastic wrapped, grated-weeks-ago stuff.

Here's how to make that salad dressing in the bowl. Chop

or mince garlic, ½ to 1 tablespoon per person, and put it in a wooden salad bowl. Add 1 tablespoon really good olive oil per person. I like California's "O" and the Italian "Ravida." Add good sea salt and freshly cracked pepper. Done! Or sometimes I add to the oil vinegar (champagne or balsamic), sometimes a pinch of sugar, sometimes ½ to 1 teaspoon Dijon mustard. That's it. Please note, the ingredients make the dish. They must be fresh so they're packed with flavor. Get the best. Get organic because the taste is richer, more pungent, and cleaner. The trick to a great salad is the toss. Add your greens—arugula or spinach or leaf lettuce, all my favorites—and toss until all the leaves are coated with the dressing, and all the ingredients are equally dispersed.

SUMMER PASTA MARINARA

Another favorite meal of mine is pasta—so many variations and so easy. First put your pot of water on to boil. Then get out your ingredients—for instance, garlic, olive oil, basil, tomatoes, and the pasta. This is a simple, clean pasta, but only for the summer when the tomatoes are good. Sauté the garlic and tomatoes in the olive oil, add a little sea salt, and cracked pepper. Do this fresh as the pasta cooks, which takes about seven minutes. Drain and add the cooked pasta to the pan, top with fresh basil, add a little grated Parmigiano Reggiano, and enjoy!

PASTA WITH ARTICHOKES

Another pasta combination is artichoke hearts, fresh when in season or canned from Whole Foods (they are the best), pine nuts, and Parmigiano Reggiano. These three flavors, along with garlic and olive oil, offer a rich, nutty taste. Put your pot of water on to boil, add minced or chopped garlic to your good olive oil in a pan, and let the garlic infuse with the oil over low heat. Then to the pan add your artichoke hearts, about three or four per person. Add a teaspoon of the pine nuts per person. Use tongs to remove the pasta from the water, and toss all the ingredients right in the pan. Then top with freshly grated parmigiano—quick and beautiful!

To any pasta you can add meats or fish, if you like, such as shrimp or sausage. Use your imagination and have fun. Add chicken to the artichoke pasta, or sausage to the fresh tomato sauce, but remember we really don't need all that meat.

PASTA WITH FRESH HERBS

Here's a light and refreshing pasta dish. Sauté garlic in olive oil and get the pasta boiling on the stove. Meanwhile, chop up lots of fresh herbs—dill, parsley, and basil. I love lots of dill with this dish. Then when the pasta is done, al dente, with tongs place it in the pan with the garlic and olive oil. Add a good squeeze of lemon, and the fresh herbs. Toss it all right in the warm pan. Grate and top it all off with the king of cheeses, Parmigiano Reggiano. A little salad, a glass of Pinot Grigio, and you're serving a twenty-minute slice of heaven.

Do not eat bread with pasta or potato dishes. This is bad food combining that will increase your glycemic index, your glucose, to uncomfortable levels. Bad food combining includes: two or more starches eaten at the same time; more than one protein eaten at the same time; and, of course, starch and protein at the same time. Ugh! It makes me feel fat and tired just imagining it. All that heavy, glopped-up food enters your digestive system like a sludge slowly churning into rock-hard cement. Imagine trying to pass that in your morning constitutional.

SMOKED SALMON WITH TOMATOES AND ROASTED ASPARAGUS

Another quick and satisfying meal that is easy to fix is smoked salmon with sliced onions, capers, and a wedge of lemon. Add a few cherry tomatoes, a hard-boiled egg, and maybe some roasted asparagus. You have all these ingredients on hand. All you have to do is plate them with style.

ROASTED VEGETABLES

Here's how to roast a vegetable, be it potatoes and squash, or asparagus. Cut the heavier, denser vegetables like potatoes, parsnips, carrots, or squash into even pieces. The green vegetables usually do not need cutting. Lay the vegetables out on a cookie pan, drizzle them with olive oil and sprinkle them with sea salt and fresh cracked pepper. Roast uncovered in a preheated oven at 425 degrees for about 20 minutes for the green vegetables, and about 40 minutes for the denser vegetables. Tomatoes, peppers, and tomatillos are all good roasted and lay the foundation for great taste treats like green chili, salsas, Harissa sauce (a wonderful North African sauce made with roasted red peppers, garlic, dried chilies, caraway seeds, salt, and olive oil) and Mexican dishes such as chili relleno. Such simple little things to do, but such a great big taste!

PAN-ROASTED PEPPERS WITH SAUSAGE

Here's a one-pan meal I like to prepare for guests because it is so easy and inexpensive. Serve it with a salad like the one above and a good, fresh crusty French bread. Splurge with the bread because your guests will love it, but you don't need to eat it while on your own. All you do is sauté 6 small Yukon Gold potatoes in a pan with olive oil, 1 large onion, ½ yellow pepper, ½ red pepper, and ½ green pepper, all for color and sweetness. Add salt and pepper to taste, and add your prepared sausage. I get Whole Foods sausage prepared from humanely raised pork. Try sausage with a little spice and heat, like chorizo or spicy Italian. Pour a good marinara sauce all over the ingredients, let the flavors marry in the pan, and serve. So good, so easy!

HOMEMADE PIZZA

Pizza is fun and simple. This spring while visiting Franci—a new mother and jewelry designer with a wonderful husband,

two dogs, two horses, and a catering business—she made us
the most delicious pizza. She bought the ready-made pizza
dough at Whole Foods, rolled it out, and topped it with tomato
sauce, mozzarella cheese, and asparagus. It was so good and
fresh. Make up your own toppings, have the kids pitch in, and
have some fun in the kitchen.

GREENS 'N' BEANS SOUP

Soups can be quick and easy, too. Here's one of my favorites. I
got the basic idea for it from Rachel Ray on the Food Channel.
Cover the bottom of your soup pot with olive oil; chop onion
and slowly let the onion become translucent. Add chopped
garlic to the pan. Do not brown the garlic because it ruins the
flavor (so add the garlic after the onions start to become translucent). Then add about 4 cups chopped greens of your choice:
Swiss chard, collards, spinach, or arugula. They should fill
the pot. Add a little salt and pepper, and let the greens cook
down to about one-quarter of their original size. I like to add
soy-based bacon bits for a subtle, smoky flavor. Then add a
15-ounce can of cannellini beans along with the juices and let

the flavors simmer a bit. Finally, stir in 1 quart of chicken or vegetable stock. This takes no time at all. Everything can be kept in your pantry, and the soup is delicious. Sometimes I add pasta for a heartier dish. So good!

OKISUKI

Another quick soup is Japanese fish stew, or okisuki. First, make your Japanese stock with 6 cups water, 1 large piece of kombu seaweed, 1 cup bonito fish flakes, ½ cup Mirin, a slice of ginger, and 2 teaspoons of salt. After that has steeped for about 10 minutes, pour it over a fine mesh sieve to render a clear broth. This is the fastest soup stock to make. Then all you do is add what you wish in the seafood department—shrimp, crab, scallops, whitefish, flounder, salmon. It doesn't matter; just add what you like. I keep it simple with only three different fish flavors at a time. Simmer for about another 10 minutes until the fish is cooked through. Add snow peas, spring onion, and perhaps some cabbage, if you like. Serve with rice, or add rice or soba noodles to the pot. Use your imagination. Learning to prepare a varied menu at home can be fun and freeing.

Here are a few more salads that I never stop enjoying.

GORGONZOLA, WALNUT, AND BEET SALAD

Combine greens (such as arugula or leaf lettuce), red onion or
shallots, McCutcheon's pickled beets, Mountain Gorgonzola,
and toasted walnuts. The dressing in the bowl is the same as
on page 130 with added balsamic vinegar, Dijon mustard, and
a little sugar. Throw it all together in the wooden bowl with
the dressing in the bottom and toss until well distributed.

SHRIMP AND AVOCADO SALAD WITH
LIME AND HABANERO CHILIES

Another salad combines the same basic dressing (olive oil,
garlic, salt and pepper), shrimp, a little lime, and habanero
chilies. After having prepared the dressing in the bottom of
the bowl, add your leaf lettuce or Romaine, and then add
shrimp and avocado that you've sautéed in olive oil, lime, and
the chilies. Pretty fancy for a few minutes' prep! Hint: I keep
frozen shrimp in the freezer in individual serving bags, then
thaw a bag in tap water for about 20 minutes. I thaw an individual serving of fish the same way.

SALAD NIÇOISE

Salad Niçoise is an old-time favorite. Basic dressing mixed right in the bowl: olive oil, garlic, vinegar, a little Dijon, sea salt, cracked pepper, and a little lemon for brightening the flavor. Then add the greens and toss. Place the salad in the center of the plate, and surround it with blanched green beans, one hard-boiled egg per person cut into quarters, a tasty tomato quartered or cherry tomatoes, fresh tuna seared with olive oil, and cracked pepper and sea salt. Remember, it's the ingredients that make the dish. Canned tuna can be used, but to make it special, maybe to serve to guests, definitely use fresh tuna.

MEDITERRANEAN GREEK SALAD

Another favorite uses the same basic dressing, leaf lettuce, feta cheese (get good feta; I like the French Valbresso sheep's feta), fresh summer tomatoes, cucumber, and olives Niçoise. Voilà! Greek salad!

COOKING AS ART

Using good, fresh ingredients; remembering to taste as you go; and letting the flavors mix and marry will always suffice in providing you with a worry-free, healthful, good meal. Be an artist in the kitchen, and treat your body, your mind, your spirit, your family, and your friends to fun, nourishing, flavorful, luscious, and interesting meals. In *The Artist's Way*, Julia Cameron writes, "Creativity is our true nature." So no excuses. Every one of us can be an artist in the kitchen. *Being an artist with food is one of the keys to staying fit and trim.*

QUICK FIX

No time in the middle of the day? Here's how to keep your energy up in a healthy, planned manner. Always keep raw nuts with you. They are a great, lasting energy lift. Sugar is quick to energize and quick to fall off, so you need more and more, as with caffeine. Nuts will linger and give you a steady energy. Hard-boiled eggs, veggie sticks, or yogurt are good to have around if you have a refrigerator handy. Try V-8 juice if all you have is gas-station food. Peanut butter will fill you up and give a more lasting energy; all you need is a spoon. Grapes are a wonderful breakfast or snack to have in the car while traveling, so easy and clean to eat. Look at the difference: all the above will give you from 150 to 500 calories, whereas a stop at any fast-food place will quadruple those calories and guarantee to keep you fat, tired, and broke.

If you're tired when you get home from school or work and need a pick-me-up but don't want to ruin your dinner by filling up on snack food, try these suggestions: take a walk, do yoga, or enjoy some stretching exercises. These methods of stirring up some good energy work because they stimulate, they allow fresh air into your lungs, and they open the spine and increase circulation. In the food department, try a cup of bouillon. Relax with a cocktail and a small handful of nuts; celery, radishes, and a good sea salt; or a couple of ounces of cheese. With planning and knowledge, you'll choose a light pick-me-up and feel great! The nuts will add about 170 calories, the two ounces of cheese 200 calories, and the celery and radishes 0 to 10 calories.

If you are really hungry when you get home and want to eat dinner right away, open a bottle of wine, put on some good music, and have a piece of cheese while slowly and creatively preparing a fabulous meal. Maybe take this time to value your accomplishments. Share your discoveries. Set the table with something special, like your fine china or new placemats;

always use cloth napkins, and bring out the candles. Go slowly and really register what you are doing. Be aware as you treat yourself to the slow, creative process—your artist at work—preparing a beautiful experience for you, or for you and your family and friends.

KEEPING IT INTERESTING

Develop a healthy, appreciative, and happy relationship with food. Engage with food. Discuss with the fishmonger where the fish comes from, and get some new ideas for preparation. Allow the butcher to suggest ways of grilling, roasting, and braising your choices. Or ask for new cuts, new sausages, and new ideas. A good butcher or fishmonger will have these answers. Whole Foods, for example, is where I got the idea for my sausages, potatoes, and peppers one-pan meal. Ask the produce guy what came in fresh, or how the peaches are today.

Discuss with your fellow shoppers everything from the weather to the state of the food industry. Make your trip to the market a valued community experience, something improbable at most large grocery chains. Chain-shopping is like touring an industrial warehouse, giving you little stimulation or encouragement to go home and be creative. But stores like Whole Foods give you an atmosphere of celebrating food. I often learn something new when I shop there, and I always enjoy myself. Zac knows me and tells me about new cheeses that come from far-off places. Get to know and be around people who love food. Your local farmers markets provide all of this, too, because they attract friendly communities of people who value good food—all the honest foods that tell the truth.

Go out and buy interesting foods you've never seen before. Inspect them, play with them, and look at the colors, the tastes, and the textures. I recently discovered skate, a seafood with a wonderful crablike flavor, and so cheap! I asked the fishmonger how to prepare it, and he suggested lightly dredging it in flour, salt, and pepper, and then sautéing it in browned butter. I found out online that that is the classic way to cook skate. Pick out some exotic fruits and vegetables you have never eaten before and take them home. Then cut them open, taste, smell, and experiment. Grill a peach, or roast a fig. Slice open a pomegranate and knock out all the seeds. Taste a star anise and lemongrass. Next add them to garlic, onion, and vegetables for a Thai flavor. Try a little coconut milk or peanut butter in a stir-fry for a more exotic Asian meal. Get cooking, get creative, and take control of your nutrition and your pleasures.

We all like instant gratification, that quick satisfaction of a job well done. Of course, so many worthwhile things take awhile to produce. But a great meal—a slow, lingering mouthful, a swallow of sensation, a little applause, or a few accolades at the table—and *boom*, you're gratified! And, you can repeat this every day.

PERFECT YOUR PANTRY

What helps your culinary arts is pantry perfection. You will need things handy at home in your cabinets, in your refrigerator, and in your freezer.

CABINETS

Good sea salt, like Artisan salt company's Fleur de Sel; regular salt; peppercorns and a grinder; onion; garlic; fresh olive oils from Spain, Greece, Italy, France, or California; and vinegars, such as champagne, balsamic, and rice vinegar. Stock Thai green or red curry paste, coconut milk, soy sauce, black bean sauce, and Mirin or sake for exotic Asian-style meals. Here's a hint: If you like Italian, use garlic. Add fresh ginger to the garlic, and you go Chinese. And add peanut butter or coconut milk to the garlic and the ginger, and you're in Thailand!

Every pantry should have real peanut butter, containing only two ingredients, peanuts and salt; canned beans, such as kidney, garbanzo, and cannellini; canned artichokes; tomato sauce; tomato paste; and in the winter, canned tomatoes. Also keep on hand dried mushrooms; boxed organic chicken broth good for risotto, quick soups, rice, and couscous; bouillon cubes; and canned tuna, salmon, and sardines for snacks or quick meals.

Always have potatoes, such as sweet, russet, Yukon, or yam; brown rice; and pastas, including linguini, fettuccine, macaroni, soba, and rice noodles. Include some grains, like couscous; polenta; wheat bulgar for Tabouleh, a Lebanese salad of wheat bulgur, parsley, onion, garlic, lemon, mint, chopped tomato, and olive oil; and maybe a falafel mix. Can you imagine the meals you could prepare with these ingredients? They're endless!

Here is a starter list for herbs and spices. Herbs to keep on hand include: dill, though better fresh; thyme; rosemary; basil, also better fresh; fennel seeds, great on pork; and the spices: curry; cumin; turmeric, which adds a brilliant yellow color and is good for digestion; ginger, best kept fresh or frozen, also excellent for digestion; crushed red pepper flakes; cinnamon; and nutmeg, good for anything with a little cream, like creamed spinach or mashed potatoes.

FREEZER

Frozen bananas and other frozen fruit such as strawberries, blueberries, raspberries, pineapple, and peaches, all for those wonderful morning milkshakes. I keep bread in the freezer, sliced and ready to go into the toaster; portion-sized fish and meat; frozen peas, the only frozen vegetable I eat for pea and mint risotto in Patricia Wells's cookbook; and Amy's frozen pizza, pot pies, and macaroni and cheese for rare evenings when I don't feel like doing anything but turning on the oven.

REFRIGERATOR

Fresh squeezed orange juice and soymilk for morning milkshakes. I also keep yogurt; nuts, such as walnuts, pecans, almonds, and pine nuts; real unsalted butter; eggs for a great, quick meal of scrambled eggs and asparagus—a marriage made in heaven—and hard-boiled eggs, great as snacks and good in salad dressings; Dijon mustard; lettuces; celery; radishes; carrots; and lemons. I like to have smoked salmon around, too, because it keeps and is a great, quick meal or snack. Please notice, there's no soda in my refrigerator. That reminds me, it's time to talk about liquids.

CHAPTER SEVEN

The Truth about Liquids

Drinking soda—any carbonated and sweetened drink, whether sweetened with fake sweetener or not—is like conducting a war on nutrition and health, a war on your body. Soda causes cavities and gum disease; it nullifies your palate, disabling your enjoyment of food, and it is addictive because it causes cravings and offers no lasting satisfaction. And the ultimate insult—it won't even quench your thirst! Caffeinated soda inhibits and can destroy the chance of a good night's sleep, and it causes innumerable gastric and intestinal irritations like irritable bowel syndrome.

A hardworking professional horsewoman I know lived on cigarettes and diet soda. Now she is in a wheelchair with MS and Lou Gehrig's disease. We have abused soda by drinking too much of it, and now it is abusing us and our precious lives. Remember, it is sugar and caffeine, and thus it is addicting.

So is the artificial sweetener, aspartame, one of the most controversial food additives ever introduced to the market. Aspartame cripples your taste buds so the only thing that has any taste at all is, yes, your diet soda. Think about it—if you had a product you wanted to sell to the public, wouldn't it be nice if it was addictive? And how about if this product was the only thing that gave the public, the customer, a taste surge? See how the soda industry has you over a barrel?

Tap water is good, and much better than it was thirty years ago. It's cleaner. Thirty years ago I did a little experiment. I left tap water in a glass jar for about a month. In that short time the bottom of the jar looked like an abandoned culture medium in a petri dish. A white-foaming, gaslike substance hung over a more solid mass on the bottom of the jar. I did the same thing just last month. Nothing accumulated on the bottom of the jar, and the water still looked clean. I was very glad because to me it proved that, yes, our water has improved. I am no expert. My opinion is not based on any informed research. But I know one thing for sure: our water is a darn sight healthier than soda! If you are unsure about your tap water, drink the bottled kind, or better yet, install a filter on your tap or have one in your refrigerator water dispenser. Just refill your used water bottles. Drink water. It's good for you.

A new study reveals that drinking massive amounts of water daily, like the sixty-four ounces prescribed by just about every health and diet book out there, does absolutely nothing for you. Of course, it can't hurt, but do you really want to spend half the day in the john? Who came up with this insane idea? This is what I learned at Dr. Shelton's Health School: When you eat water-based foods such as fruits and vegetables, you do not need to imbibe a lot of water. Drinking a lot of water with a meal just washes the vitamins and minerals right through your body. Could drinking volumes of water all day not do this also? Water is good, and it is a natural appetite suppressant, but as Dr. Gillian McKeith says, "Your stomach needs to be lubricated, not flooded. When you drink fluids with your meals, you drown your digestive enzymes and only partial digestion takes place." It's that old paradigm: moderation is good.

We must observe that drinking all this water has been a boon in recent decades for the water retail business: water purveyors, water excavators, water drillers? All over the world—and yes, I have drunk most of them, from France to Fiji—businesses are bottling mountain and spring water. A huge business, and we're buying it up like crazy. But do we have to? And what about all those plastic bottles? Where are they going? I say drink filtered tap water. Save yourself a fortune, save the earth, and save your body by avoiding soda.

However, don't turn to those sports drinks loaded with sugars. Be safe and drink only freshly squeezed juice. An irony has been playing out in the water and drink industry. Companies are adding vitamins and minerals to their products all in the effort to make them seem healthy and to mimic the real thing: freshly squeezed juice.

At our local grocery-store chain, I took a good look at these sports drinks and waters. Here are the results of my quick and easy research that anyone can do to confirm. Snapple, Propel, Sobe, and Glaceau "vitamin waters" all listed either sugar, high-fructose corn syrup, or cane sugar as the second ingredient after water. Remember, the ingredients of any food or drink are listed in the order of volume. In the case of vitamin waters they are mostly water and sugar, just like soda—that's what you're paying for.

Power drinks are the same. Their first listed ingredient is water, usually followed by two sugars, such as Gatorade's high-fructose syrup and then sucrose syrup. I say get the real thing, the product that is honest and doesn't lie to you. Get your vitamins and minerals from whole foods, the foods that come from the earth, not from test tubes. Drink freshly squeezed juice, add a little water and a pinch of salt, and you have your own power drink. If you can, invest in a juice squeezer because your body will thank you for this investment.

As with so many of our choices, alcoholic beverages have a good side and a bad side. On the good side, matching wine to your meal not only encourages digestion, it enhances the flavor and the experience of dining, in direct opposition to what a can of soda can do. A cocktail taken before dinner adds to relaxation and provides us with a pleasant social ritual, the cocktail hour. A well-prepared cocktail will act as an aperitif, a whetting of the appetite. Some studies have shown that alcohol taken in moderate amounts can be healthy, good for stress management, and just plain relaxing and fun. Conscientious quaffing is the key!

On the other side, the bad side, too much alcohol destroys health, emotions, and even organ function. When your use of alcohol is out of control, just as when eating is out of control, it can ruin your life. The only time I overeat is when I've had too much to drink. The alcohol lessens your resolve and inhibits conscious thinking, the thinking that leads to healthful, conscious acts. Some of the worst arguments in my life have erupted from too much drinking. I lost a very good friend one night after too much drinking. To this day I miss her.

I had driven down from Minneapolis to Columbia, Missouri, where Mary lived. It was a long drive, about six hundred miles. I was tired and hungry. Mary was still working, and I had no place to go and refresh myself. So I went to our favorite restaurant, assuming we would eat pretty soon, and then I would go to her place and collapse. Well, I had a martini to relax after the long drive. Then I had another, and she finally arrived wanting a cocktail. So we had a cocktail, and pretty soon she said she wanted to eat someplace else. I was too tired to consider this extra drive as a hazard.

We arrived at the restaurant and had another drink. I don't remember what it was, but pretty soon, what I remember is the bartender coming over and asking us to leave. We were arguing. We were loud, and Mary left.

There I was: alone, tired, and drunk, with no place to go. So I called my niece who lived not too far away, and she saved me. As I followed her home, I kept veering off the road. My niece soon put a stop to that and gathered me into her car and drove us both home to safety. Thank you, Linda!

I have not seen Mary since that incident. Our friendship ended with too many cocktails and a grievous misunderstanding of words. Loss of friendship, a loved one, maybe even a family member is just too great a price to pay for an evening's loss of composure, planning, and discipline.

Driving after consuming alcohol is just plain insane. How does anyone survive adolescence? So, again, watch out and be vigilant. Be very careful with alcohol, and leave it for social occasions, celebrations, and relaxation. Live life in joyful expression, enjoy the sensuous side, laugh a lot, and have fun. But, and this is a very large "but," notice how little alcohol you really need, and how easily this lovely source of pleasure can be abused.

Here's what I do to keep from having too many drinks and to avoid unnecessary, life-changing mishaps. First, one cocktail should last at least forty-five minutes. Give your body time to assimilate alcohol slowly so as not to shock it into drunkenness. Fast drinking is not about pleasure; it is about getting drunk. Second, always eat as you take in alcohol. Civilized drinking always includes food—for instance, the friendly cocktail hour with hors d'oeuvres and wine to enhance the subtle and varied flavors of a meal.

Another easily and often abused substance is caffeine. Watch out for this one, too, because along with sugar it is deceptive and addicting. Just notice how once you've gotten on the caffeine track, how hard it is to get off. Notice how you can hardly function without it, whether in the morning or late afternoon. Clearly these are the symptoms of ingesting an addictive substance. I regard sugar or caffeine no differently than I do drugs like cocaine or amphetamines. All are highly addictive stimulants that over time drag us down and destroy our health.

In my senior year of high school I was diagnosed with depression and given a prescription drug called Desbutal, a mixture of amphetamine and barbiturate. It contained 5 mg of methamphetamine and 30 mg of Nembutal, or pentobarbital sodium. A few years later it was taken off the market. Other drugs were prescribed, but none had the effectiveness of Desbutal. I soon realized that controlling my moods with drugs did not suit me. Their effects were obviously using me like a tool, not really curing me. My mood and energy were beholden to the drugs. My friends noticed my reactive swings in behavior. So I stopped. And then I paid attention—to me, my body, and what I put into it—I was becoming consciously aware. I began taking control over my body, my emotions, and my physiological health.

Soon I began observing the effects on me of other sources of stimulants, such as coffee and sugar. What became clear to me through reading and through trial and error was that these drinks and foods could do the same as the drugs. Maybe not as obviously but certainly enough for me to realize the powerful negative effects they had on my emotional condition. For instance, one cup of coffee stimulates me for about three hours. But soon I become tense, anxious, easily aggravated, and even paranoid. Then the next day I find I want more coffee because I am so lethargic and experiencing ennui, a feeling very close to depression. The letdown is debilitating, and the anxiety ruins my day.

Sugar does something similar, but the subtle difference is that sugar can make me feel good, even a little high. The stimulation is less apparent than with coffee and much more short-lived, so I want more sugar to keep the good feelings coming. When I stop ingesting sugar and go to bed, the morning after I am depressed, and it is very hard for me to get up the enthusiasm to carry on with the new day.

Caffeine and sugar act like drugs. They pick you up and let you down. They play with your moods. I am not a doctor, and I know these substances do not adversely affect many people, but if you are susceptible to mood swings, anxiety, or depression, I recommend you use them sparingly or leave them alone. Over the years I've learned how to eat for energy and not have to rely on drugs or stimulants to get through my beautiful day.

I admit that caffeine is great once in a while—nothing like the *New York Times* and a good cup of coffee. Honoré de Balzac, nineteenth-century French novelist, I understand, drank pots of coffee. Many writers use the stuff as a stimulus for clear, alert thinking. Creativity seems to flow, as does housework, on caffeine. However, it will addict you and make it nearly impossible for you to function without it if you take it on a regular basis—using it, in other words, like a crutch. Sounds similar to alcohol, doesn't it?

Both these pleasures, coffee and alcohol, can soon turn to nasty and debilitating—no longer really enjoyable—habits. Be aware, be conscious and thoughtful in your daily choices of what you drink. Appreciate these unneeded substances once in a while. If you do, their enjoyment will be enhanced, and you will feel so much better having control over them. Be autonomous and powerful, not a pawn of marketing or any liquid druglike substance.

Kay Redfield Jamison writes in *Exuberance: The Passion for Life*, "We are not the only species to seek high moods. Sloths intoxicate themselves by eating fermented flowers and chewing coca leaves, and elephants get high on fermented fruit and vines. Reindeer ingest hallucinogenic mushrooms, water buffaloes graze on opium poppies, and llamas and monkeys, like sloths, ingest the stimulant from coca leaves." We all seek pleasure; we all like to heighten our energy and alertness or dull them for release and sleep, and who wouldn't?

Who wouldn't want to escape and find that moment of pleasure, bliss, ease, or satisfaction through chocolate and a movie; champagne and caviar; new jewelry; a new night-gown; cold beer, chips, and your favorite football team on TV; steak, baked potato, and a Bordeaux; a cashmere robe; Hendrick's Gin with a slice of cucumber; or double choco-late mocha ice cream? Who wouldn't want to remove oneself from the drudgery, the banality, the malaise, the stress, the alienation, or just the sheer horrors of life, the worst one of all being indifference?

We all like a little pleasurable respite from sensing those negative perceptions and feelings. Sugar gives us pleasure and a little quick energy; caffeine lifts us up and makes us alert; alco-hol releases dopamine and serotonin, offering a happy high that exhilarates and disinhibits. But boy, do these pleasures plummet you to the deepest, lowest lows if used without good judgment and moderation. "External sources of exuberance are ultimately overruled by the brain's inclination to seek out equilibrium" (Jamison). Hence, the fall is inevitable, painful, and far.

Equilibrium: This is what we lose by being disengaged from nature—by fearing nature, really—and not knowing our habitat, our environment, not honoring it, not reveling in it. The result for us is imbalance. Equilibrium is what we lose by not being in the presence of art, the great balancer. Music, dance, painting and art museums, opera—each participated in, or observed, or listened to on a weekly, if not a daily, basis will help us all regain equilibrium. We have lost connection to our space and our place, all the life in that space, and a celebration of that space—our planet. This is imbalance.

We have also lost community and the energy to engage with and within our space/place. We've reached an imbalance, making ourselves feel deep dissatisfaction and alienation. We live on hallowed ground as do all the other life forces we share the planet with: animals, plants, rocks, minerals, electricity, motion, gravity—all requiring balance and harmony. In *Sugar Blues*, William Dufty asks, quoting Chief Seattle to President Franklin Pierce in 1855, "What is man without the beasts? If all the beasts were gone, men would die from great loneliness of spirit, for whatever happens to the beast also happens to man. All things are connected"—a prescient statement foreseeing our present-day alienation and our solitude because of our lack of connection with other life forms and forces.

It's time we celebrate and find joy in our existence, expressing this joy with gratitude for the body/vehicle that transports
us through this beautiful maze of atoms, forming potential,
possibility, and equilibrium. We can reclaim equilibrium,
community, and balance through autonomous thinking, and
healthy and conscious living. Enjoy your moments of pleasure, for you deserve them, but remember to honor balance
and equilibrium, boundaries, planning and management, and
exuberance. Enjoy and listen to these excerpts from Jamison's
wonderful book, *Exuberance: The Passion for Life*:

> Exuberance is an abounding, ebullient, effer-
> vescent emotion. It is kinetic and unrestrained,
> joyful, irrepressible. It is not happiness, although
> they share a border. It is instead, at its core, a more
> restless, billowing state.
>
> Psychologists, who in recent years have taken
> up the study of positive emotions, find that joy
> widens one's view of the world and expands imag-
> inative thought.
>
> [President Theodore Roosevelt's exuberance],
> his magnetic force, said one observer, "surrounded

him as a kind of nimbus, imperceptible but irresistibly drawing to him everyone who came into his presence." Roosevelt used his infectious enthusiasm, which was tethered to a highly disciplined intelligence, to render unprecedented reform through actions of the federal government. Nowhere was this more obvious and lasting than in his drive to conserve the American wilderness.

Roosevelt's passion was our space, this planet.

Just a little side note about passion. It will fill you, engage you, and satisfy you like no substance on earth. Find out what you believe in and care about the most. Passion is the driving force behind all that is exciting in life: exploration of the universe, pursuing physics, writing poetry, studying life, writing symphonies and conducting them, playing a musical instrument, doing mathematics, singing and dancing, creating art, saving the world and its animals, helping the sick and the elderly, teaching the young, serving God, and serving mankind. We are born to certain heights. It is our job to ferret them out for ourselves and follow the path. Believe that when you are driven by passion to seek, to learn, and serve, you have very little time for sluggish mornings due to drinking too many sugared sodas, too much alcohol, too much caffeine, or any other drugs.

I raise my glass to you and your passion to think, feel, imagine, do, and contribute.

Santé! To your health!

CHAPTER EIGHT

Know Your Power

Before and during the writing of this book, I have been asking myself several questions: *How was I able to conquer overeating? What made me able to change my thinking and my habits? How did I succeed?* And, in particular, *why do so many fail?* I know I am no better than the next person. I know I had and have some of the same thinking patterns as other overweight people.

I thought of myself as fat and incapable. I no longer see myself that way. I thought about food all the time. I still do. I used to say, "If I look at a doughnut, I gain weight." I was depressed and got very little exercise. I have since learned that for me exercise along with honest eating habits staves off depression. I also discovered that moving the body stimulates the brain, energizes me, and is a key aid to digestion. In turn, digestion is key to weight loss and maintenance.

Think of it as a daily circle in motion—you eat, you move, your brain is energized, your organs move, you digest food, and you eat again. Keep the motion. Activity like my daily walks with Chaps, my "Stretch and Strengthen" exercise tape I've been doing for nearly thirty years, and the fact that I have a sport I engage in at least four times a week all serve to keep me moving. So movement is key to healthy success.

Actually, I have to recognize another contributing factor. I have removed myself from an environment that induced my overeating. After I left home my weight control became easier. I do not know why. But I do know that an unhealthy environment, one that is indifferent to your particular suffering and of little help in assuaging it, can make it very difficult to overcome any weakness. We are creatures who like familiarity and easy survival. If our lives are easy and comfortable in a place, we don't always recognize nor do we analyze how or why it may be making us weak and sick to live there. Sometimes we misunderstand these driving survival forces that come from within. We may choose what is bad for us because it is familiar.

Take an honest look at your circumstances and see if they have any influence on your overeating. If they do, either change them, or if that is impossible recognize the difficulty, accept it with conscious awareness, and in turn you will weaken this destructive force of circumstances. These two huge things have enabled me to engage with food on a healthy basis: exercise that I enjoy and look forward to, and removing myself from an unsupportive environment.

But what was it that got me over the seemingly insurmountable hump, the diet hump? I define the diet hump as an endless trial of success and failure; many may call it "on and off the wagon." Today I have no "wagon" in my life, and there doesn't need to be one in yours. I believe my autonomous thinking and my curiosity helped me get rid of that on-and-off-the-wagon cycle. My success results from years of independent experimenting, research, and observation, all stirred by independent thinking and curiosity.

Vanity helps, no doubt. I like to look and feel good. Really enjoying food also helps. I love to eat, prepare, read about,

search for, and purchase food. I have never liked being controlled. I refuse to be a pawn of the system. These are active
and powerful considerations.

But what was it *really* that changed my attitude and my
engagement with food?

The fact that I did it on my own. I did not prevail when I went
on diets like Weight Watchers or any other program telling me
what to do. They work for the short term and can be educa-
tional. However, within a diet's boundaries I never had to think
for myself. Plus, the diet or program builds the wagon; you are
either on it or off it. In order to change a habit for good, you
must observe what needs to be changed, accept what needs to
be changed, think for yourself, and change it all on your own.
See it and do it for yourself. Take action. Make mistakes, learn
from them, and continue on taking action to improve yourself.
Julia Cameron quotes F. W. Goethe, "Action has magic, grace,
and power in it." Yes, get help figuring things out—this I did
and still do. But in the end it is all up to you. Only you have the
power to live your life the way you want.

I did not like being fat. I researched, read, tried, failed, listened, watched, learned, analyzed, deleted bad information,

and always kept good information and observations in my head and in my journal. If a friend of mine did not have any eating issues, I watched how she ate, how she prepared her meals, and even observed how she thought about food. I remember my friend Linda preparing lunch for us in her home when we were in high school. At the red kitchen counter she included things that I thought I had to stay away from—beans, cheese, and mayonnaise. I then realized that her salad with kidney beans, blue cheese, and vegetables was not only good but also nutritious and satisfying. Another lunch she made for us was a tuna fish salad sandwich on toast with sliced tomatoes. Using real mayonnaise and fresh summer tomatoes and taking the time to toast the bread just made it so fresh and good. I can still feel the warm bread against the cool tomatoes in my mouth. That sandwich was so satisfying; it was memorable. Eating with real satisfaction is key to health.

A real satisfying meal—how many of us reach that level of fullness and satisfaction today, given our tasteless, card-board-encased, overly salted, prepared, and takeout foods? We're never really satisfied. Why? Because we're not doing anything for ourselves. We are not taking any action. We're not preparing ourselves enjoyable and satisfying meals. And we're not educating ourselves about food and the atrocities in the food industry that are harming not only ourselves, but our farmed animals as well. Every day I see thousands of people buying factory-farmed food. People lining up at fast-food joints, people shopping at grocery-store chains, and people eating at franchise restaurants—all, or most, of which prepare and sell factory-farmed animal products. *Take action*—stop buying it. You'll feel better about yourself, and the animals trapped in this nightmarish business will find some relief.

Food has become a convenience—not something to be savored, not something to aid our health and success in life, but a nuisance that we must hurry through and get over with. To do what? Sit in front of the computer, the TV, or work after hours? What is everyone doing that is so much more important than enjoying good meals, our most immediate source of good health? I ask you, what is more important than the health of your body, your only vehicle through life? And why not enjoy this lovely, varied, luscious health source we have?

What is this lovely source? Simple good food, the food that tells us the truth, the food that is what it says it is: a real banana, real eggs from chickens produced without cages and antibiotics, and real lettuce, not some bioengineered facsimile made in a test tube. Be autonomous, be curious, ask tough questions about what you eat and drink, and educate yourself. Create self-empowerment through action—that magical action. These actions are crucial for success. Autonomous thinking, curiosity, and self-empowerment: every day these tools enable my triumph over depression and overeating.

Remember the power of the brain as it visualizes the food you plan to eat. The American diet with its glopped-up, gooey food disgusts me. That's the shift I've developed in my brain. Do whatever it takes for you, too, to see that plate of heaped-up greasy meats and cheeses on soggy fat-laden bread as something intolerable for you to put in your mouth. See gooped-up, gooey desserts as nothing but addictive, gut-rotting sludge in your body, clogging your arteries, depleting your energy, and distracting your will to live happily.

The American diet is deceptive, not honest. Look to clean, honest, and unadulterated foods such as fresh, organic raspberries with a little cream; cantaloupe with a little salt and freshly squeezed lime juice; fresh, crisp celery and radishes with sea

salt; fresh fish; tasty organic chicken; green vegetables fresh
from the farmers market; and a variety of crisp lettuces ready
for an imported Italian olive oil, Parmigiano Reggiano, garlic .
. . oh, I could go on and on! Eat clean, honest food, and you will
learn to love yourself and consequently empower yourself.

"Empower" means to invest with power, or to equip with
supply or ability, and to enable. Empowerment means to
invest with authority. This is what I want each and every one
of us to have: Authority over ourselves. Authority over what
we eat. Authority over our lives.

Last night Tom said, "We vote with our dollars." Every
time you do not buy bad, dishonest food, you register a vote
against it. Every time you buy healthy, organic, good food,
you register a vote for it. This is your power.

We've looked at calories and the inevitable equation of
energy in and energy out. I've provided you with the analogy of calories as money. You only have so many calories to
spend in your health checkbook. I have 1800 to 2000 a day,
for example. If you spend too much and go over your budget,
you will gain weight. If you are frugal and spend less than you
have in your calorie budget, you will lose weight.

We've searched the dark hallways of ourselves and found some answers to the big question: why do we overeat? Food is so convenient, so soothing, and so good, it enables us to forget our pain. But, recognizing our pain, our Achilles heel, releases us from the bondage of shame, guilt, ill health, and even depression. Acceptance weakens the demons. We accept our human imperfection and carry on.

So what if we incur little or even giant infringements on our health plan? We know our calories, so we adjust the next meal or the next day. We know ourselves, so we forgive and forget because we're worth it. And we've brought together three helpful tools—a calorie counter, a mirror, and a journal—and we know how to use them to personalize the changes we want to make.

As we have come to know ourselves a little better, we have also come to know and understand our precious workhorse-like bodies. We've looked at food combinations that work for our bodies and food combinations that work against them. We've looked at what debilitates our digestive system and turns to sludgy cement along that long, complicated track. We've looked at the foods that lie and the foods that tell the truth. We've gone on a food discovery. I hope it's the beginning of a discovery that excites you about all the luscious and wonderful delights that are out there and that are good to eat. We all have a creative side. Find the artist/chef inside you. Explore food; ask questions of your butcher, fishmonger, and produce person. Delight in food and satisfy yourself.

Most of all, know your power. Stop being a victim of the profit-over-health-driven food industry. Equally as important, stop being a victim of time that drives you to eat fast, and drives you to eat fast food. Remember, the food industry is, in Kessler's words, "the manipulator of the consumers' minds and desires ... Heinz, PepsiCo, the National Pork Board, Smucker's, and Tyson focus on consumers whose lives are increasingly harried ... feeling more stress ... who say their responsibilities can be overwhelming." Stop to consider, then slow down.

Control your life through conscious awareness and creative planning. Wake up, America, and look at yourself and all the beautiful food that comes from our earth, the trees, the soil, and the seas. Plan what you will eat, and stop spontaneous feedings resulting in bad food. Celebrate your body, your power, and your life through autonomous action, the magical action that has grace and power in it. Enjoy the bounty. Enjoy your life.

In my good-bye paragraph I want to share with you what enabled the writing of this book. It is the very thing that enabled me to overcome emotionally driven overeating. It is what enabled me to find my proper life and live it. And everyone has it.

But first, from William Wordsworth's "Ode, Intimations of Immortality from Recollections of Early Childhood" (1807):

> Our birth is but a sleep and a forgetting:
> The Soul that rises with us, our life's Star,
>> Hath had elsewhere its setting,
>> And cometh from afar:
>> Not in entire forgetfulness,
>> And not in utter nakedness,
> But trailing clouds of glory do we come
>> From God, who is our home. (v.58–65)

We all trail clouds of glory upon birth. We come into this world with a passion or many passions. So what is it that enabled me to conquer depression and overeating? I reclaimed my passion, my true soul, my "life's star." I reclaimed my natural love of life and my exuberance. So, again, find your passion, reclaim it, act upon it despite your fear, and follow it with determination, persistence, resilience, and optimism. If I did it, so can you. Go for it with exuberance!

SOURCES

FOOD AND DIET

Goulding, Matt, and David Zinczenko. *Eat This, Not That*. Rodale, 2009.

Guiliano, Mireille. *French Women Don't Get Fat*. Knopf, 2005.

Lappé, Frances Moore. *Diet for a Small Planet*. Random House, 1971 (repr. 1991).

McKeith, Gillian. *You Are What You Eat*. Plume, 2006.

McKenna, Paul. *I Can Make You Thin*. Sterling, 2007.

Robertson, Laurel, Carol Flinders, and Brian Ruppenthal. *The New Laurel's Kitchen*. Ten Speed Press, 1976 (repr. 1986).

HEALTH

Dufty, William. *Sugar Blues*. Warner Books, 1976.

Fuhrman, Joel. *Fasting and Eating for Health*. St. Martin's Press, 1998.

Shelton, Herbert M. *Food Combining Made Easy*. Dr. Shelton's Health School, 1951.

COOKBOOKS

Olney, Richard. *Simple French Food*. Simon and Schuster, 1974.

Simonds, Nina. *Spoonful of Ginger*. Knopf, 1999.

Waters, Alice. *The Art of Simple Food*. Random House, 2007.

———. *Chez Panisse Café Cookbook*, HarperCollins, 1999.

Wells, Patricia. *Vegetable Harvest*. HarperCollins, 2007.

FOOD AND FOOD INDUSTRY

Campbell, T. Colin. *The China Study*. Benbella Books, 2005.

Food Inc. Robert Kenner, director. Michael Pollan, consultant. Participant Media Production, 2008.

Kessler, David A. *The End of Overeating*. Rodale, 2009.

Pollan, Michael. *In Defense of Food*, Penguin Group, 2008.

———. *The Omnivore's Dilemma*. Penguin Group, 2007.

Robbins, John. *The Food Revolution: How Your Diet Can Help Save Your Life and Our Planet*. Red Wheel/Weiser, 2001.

LIFE

Cameron, Julia. *The Artist's Way*. Penguin, 2002.

Jamison, Kay Redfield. *Exuberance: The Passion for Life*. Random House, 2004.

———. *An Unquiet Mind: A Memoir of Moods and Madness*. Random House, 1995.

Orloff, Judith. *Positive Energy*. Harmony Books, 2004.

Tolle, Eckhart. *A New Earth*. Plume, 2006.

———. *The Power of Now*, Namaste Publishing, 1997.

WEB SITES

Chowbaby.com

Eatwellguide.org

Eatwild.com

Slowfood.com